STANDING
IN GAPS
A MEMOIR

Seamus O'Rourke

BIG GUERILLA PRESS

Seamus O'Rourke
Druminchingore
Newtowngore
Co.Leitrim
www.seamusorourke.com

Publisher's Note: This is partly a work of fiction. Names, characters, places, and incidents may be a product of the author's imagination. Locales and public names are sometimes used for atmospheric purposes. Any resemblance to actual people, living or dead, or to businesses, companies, events, institutions, or locales is completely on purpose.

Book Layout ©2017 BookDesignTemplates.com

Cover Design by Ronan Ward | Homebird Design, Cavan. www.homebirddesign.ie

Printed by Turloch Dolan harvestmoon print and design www.harvestmoonprinting.com

Standing in Gaps/ Seamus O'Rourke. – 2nd ed.
ISBN 978-1-5272-6597-4

To Mammy

Pauline O'Rourke

She'd have the whole work done while
you'd be unbuttoning your coat.

Contents

Prologue

I'm writing this memoir in the summer of 2020. I had set this time aside to try and write a light-hearted account of my early life. Then in March this year, the Corona Virus hit and the world was put on lockdown. Everything stopped. Hundreds of thousands of lives have been lost and families all over the world have been devastated. Maybe it's not the time for light-hearted prose – or maybe it's now, more than ever, important to search for the light and the light-hearted. These pages are about family and people and time – written in a time when everything stood still – about a time when everything moved slowly – in Leitrim of the '60's, '70's and '80's – that means real slow. So slow, I've had to put a bit of a skin on it, to make it sit up on the page. But it's all here, I think – the first eighteen years of my life.

I was born on the 11th March 1965, I know that for a fact and I came a couple of weeks early, so I'm fairly sure that I was conceived on the 23rd of June 1964; a Tuesday – that was the start of it. It was my mother's birthday and the Auld Lad had forgotten her birthday, he always did, but made up for it that night in the room upstairs beside the landing. I'd say about half ten after the news, he swung in his big hydraulic populator and him and her took into making me. My mother had just turned twenty-two, he was gone thirty-seven. He was fierce fond of me mother, especially after the news and when the bed got warmed up. The 'old' house would have shook with the tremor of birthday joisting above in the room and that house was well shook already with the makings of my older siblings; Margaret and Kevin. Squeezed out in a hurry, to stand in gaps and help 'do the things'. But this night was all about me. Of course, I can't honestly say what went on between the sheets that night, but it was probably spectacular – incongruous, yes and fairly quick I'd say, but in some hot and sticky way – spectacular.

By the way – I know I shouldn't be dealing in probability here, it's a memoir after all. Let's deal with the facts, says you. Well, you see, if I'm being totally honest – not much really happened me – ever! I was born in Leitrim, where the art of dodging about unnoticed is a fifty-five-year degree course. The core of this memoir will have to be massaged a little to bring out the juices. I wanted to tell a story of - mystery and mayhem - courage and corruption - triumph and failure... and loads of drunken sex. That's what a well-worn life should be. Well, I'm not one of 'The Rolling Stones'. I haven't much to say about success and high living – I didn't drink till I was twenty, so there'll be no drunken sex and although there's lots of failure – it's not very spectacular, it's just coming up short at fairly regular intervals. In essence, I'm a plain loaf – a barmbrack without the fruit – my life, as forgettable as an early Mass in the middle of lent. But that won't stop me. I know somewhere inside of me, there's a presentable memoir. Exciting and bold? – well maybe not, but there's nothing stopping it from being mildly funny and the strange thing is, the more honest I am, the funnier it gets. From far away, Leitrim looks small and our lives insignificant. Not enough there to fill out the pages of a fairly thick book. Well, come closer and I'll show ya!

And remember – it's not a memory test – who cares what I can remember? I just want to tell about the misery and the fun we had. It was all around me – in the fields and houses, in the people and the time. This was my time and what a time it was, if you had nothing better to be at.

CHAPTER 1

The Corner Bar

My father sat with Christy Mimna in a small bar beside the hospital in Manorhamilton. It was eleven o'clock in the morning on the 11th of March 1965. My father was Jim Rourke. He was a relieved man. Relieved that he was able to 'treat' Christy to a few drinks and him after bringing me mother all this way. Christy had driven them the fifty-seven miles from south Leitrim, because our car was in Brewster's garage in Carrigallen, getting serviced. The Auld Lad left it in the day before, ten days before I was due, but Mammy's waters broke the following morning and so Daddy went up the road to his first cousin for help. Christy said he'd drive to Manorhamilton, of course he would and they set off. They almost forgot to pick up Mammy at the house, they were that excited, although it was her was having the baby. They also picked up Christy's sister, Peggy in Gortahose, a mile into the journey – company for my mother and more importantly, another woman, to talk to Mammy about woman's things.

'The Corner Bar' was empty that morning. A roundy shouldered fella by the name of John had just opened up. He had a white shirt and braces. He wasn't the owner, far too oblivious for that. He grabbed them two bottles of beer and two half ones, took my father's money, but showed no interest in their plight or business and then proceeded to slap a mop around the floor. As unwelcoming and as brazen as you like – no way to treat a father and godfather to be.

The ambience, circumstance and time of day were not conducive to normal pub talk and so the two men sat in silence mostly. My father, every now and then, stretching his long neck to look out the window – to check on the car outside – making sure that Mammy was alright and still sitting up in the back, chatting.

This scene and these men might seem callous and neglectful, but we must remember the time. Back then, it was only common courtesy to bring a lad for a drink and him after doing you a favour. Back then, there was no flapping about when someone was having a baby. My mother would have been just as anxious as my father to 'treat' Christy for his kind intervention and all the better with her sitting outside. At least this way, there was a limit on how long the men would stay. If they had dropped her off first – they may have stayed longer in the pub and spent more. And as it was her third child, my twenty-two year old mother was a veteran baby popper and well able to give the window a tap if things started to move. She was a pocket-rocket, as hardy a bit of stuff as ever came about Drumshangore – and Drumshangore had some tough ones there already.

When my parents got married in 1960 – they were an unlikely couple. She was eighteen and five-foot-two – he was six-foot-three and thirty-three. Separated by fifteen years and thirteen inches – yet it worked, they hardly ever had a row. She looked up to him. He looked down on no one. Their love was discreet. No rubbing or hugging or petting and I only saw them dance on one occasion – at a Dinner Dance – an ungainly affair. The Auld Lad looked like he was carrying a wet bag of cement and didn't know where to leave it down. Mostly, they played the part of obliging neighbours. Him, lucky to get one so young – her, lucky to get someone so near hand. They had the four of us, Margaret and Kevin and then me. My younger sister Geraldine would come along three years later. Two boys, two girls, a few acres of the poor, wet Leitrim ground and enough common sense to feed a nation.

My father stared at a ceramic figurine that sat on a crowded shelf behind the counter of the Corner Bar. It was a Gaelic footballer wearing green and yellow and standing on a plinth which read – LEITRIM. It somehow gave him a jag of realism, reminded him of who he was and where he was. It prompted a story – my father talked best in stories or yarns or good ones. Adam Brewster had told him this one the day before when he was leaving in the car.

The Brewster brothers, Adam; Jack and Jim were well renowned for their mechanical and intellectual offerings, aimed at a certain brethren who craved learning beyond the pulpit and the pale. The brothers were educated and thoughtful. They had poise and were pompous enough to assume a role of prophet and preacher among the unenlightened. Their garage was a Mecca to the smart alec and the lazy. Brewster's story was of course, in the form of a parable:

"If a man has a flaw – he will always have something that will compensate for that flaw. It may not be apparent, but it's there. If a man has bad sight, his hearing might be better than most. If he has a speech impediment, he may sing like a thrush. Or, if he has a short leg, the other one will, more than likely be long".

Christy threw back his head and laughed goodo. The fact that the yarn came from a Brewster, gave it extra credence and with that, gave him a confidence to overindulge in his reaction. Suddenly the laughing stopped. It was me. Christy noticed commotion outside in the car. The women were getting restless. Something was astir – yes – me. The men drank up and said thanks to John. John didn't answer or care. Christy told him they were going up to the hospital – that there was a pair of women outside in the car and one of them was going to have a baby. John still didn't care. He didn't give two hoots about Christy or my father or the two women and certainly not about some unborn baby – even if that unborn baby was me.

My mother was dropped to the hospital a couple of hundred yards up the road. My Aunt – another Peggy, my father's sister, was a nurse and midwife there. She was the kindest and most laidback of all the Rourkes – a feat in itself, as most of my father's crowd marched to a slow air. Mammy carried a straw shopping bag with her things; a nightdress, a bit of knitting in case there was a lull and a small bottle of holy water. The holy water was not her idea. Aunt Peggy took her hand, smiled her warmest smile and said, *"Now"*. And that was it – time for my mother to go and have me – time for the Auld Lad to go home and do the things. There was some nodding and bashfulness as they said goodbye and then my father and his crew made for home, in time for milking and feeding calves and taking back the day.

As they passed the Corner Bar, John was outside sweeping the sidewalk. His shirt as white as his sunken brow. Was he deep in thought, or just dazed by daylight? My father studied him. Here was a man simply going about his daily work – dividing his morning into strokes of a well-worn twig. It was hard to believe that this man had kith or kin. Hard to imagine him at the head of the table cutting bread. But whatever it was, the burden of his plight seemed to weigh heavy on his rounded frame. My father sought answers in the eyes of men like John. How did this world come up so shy for him? Why did it come up so shy for so many?

My father was a bright man; he left school early, but had untapped reservoirs of wisdom and understanding.

His own brush-strokes though, were light and tentative – his course now charted and followed slow. Inside, the left-over's of a dreamer, a fantasiser who ran into reality. He'd had his fling and so today, a Thursday in March 1965, he was simply thoughtful. The pillar of our family till the day he died and beyond.

Christy and his sister were giddy company on the way home from the hospital. It was a Mimna trait, to find fun in the empty spaces left behind by others. Their family was a tonic – as childish and playful as they could be candid and resourceful. The Father-to-be was composed. He yawned his out loud yawn. A yawn that said, *'This child will make three and I'm only getting used to one'*. And then his mind wandered. His wife, Pauline was going to be okay and Peggy, his sister was there. His wisdom and understanding were not required in the maternity ward. His time better spent at home. Christy drew him out – asked about names for the baby, came up with some rare ones – said French names were in, said *"Ooh la la"* and laughed goodo. Daddy only talked about the road and the great straight stretch between Drumkeeran and Drumshanbo, the bendy bit they called the Devil's Elbow and then the ever increasing pot-holes as they came close to Drumshangore. Granny would be waiting there.

My granny was Margaret O'Rourke – she added the 'O' when she married my grandfather. She was at home minding my brother and sister. A fierce proud, strong woman. She and my mother locked horns on more than one occasion, neither saying outright what was on their mind; neither giving any ground. Granny ruled the roost for now. She didn't go the easy-going nature of the Rourkes. She was nee Kiernan from deepest Drumreilly, the neighbouring half parish; fiercest of rivals and where we often went for our women. No woman could stand in a gap or pitch hay like a Drumreilly woman. She had married my grandfather, Michael Rourke in an arranged marriage. She had come back from America and he had no woman – so, someone put two and two together and came up with grandparents for me. He was much older and a bit soft, not slow – soft – was caught one time reading a book and he used to play the fiddle. *'Books and fiddles won't grow oats or tie down hay'*. That was her philosophy and no one was going to argue. She was standing at the back door when my father sauntered up the lane, his demeanour the same, whether my mother had just given birth to triplets or if it had been nothing only wind. *"Well?"* Granny asked. *"Anything happening?"*. *"No, nothing yet"*, was my father's reply.

CHAPTER 2

Doing the Things

My father sat on the bed for a minute. He was just home from delivering my mother to the hospital. He was still in his good clothes. Despite the commotion of the morning – my mother's unseemly behaviour at the byre door when her waters broke – the footherin' about with creamery cans when the auld lad got excited and the arranging of alternative transport, he still had time to put on his good clothes. He never went beyond the end of the lane in his old duds. Always respectable, always well dressed, always clean. But now he had to do the things. There was an evening's work ahead and he had to summon the will from somewhere and climb back into those same old duds left abandoned on the floor. Not so easy, with the few drinks from the Corner Bar and the slight hint of celebration in the air. He looked around the lonely room. A bed, a dressing table, a clotheshorse and a wooden chest – that was it. There was a wardrobe out on the landing beside the chimney breast. Tonight, he would sleep alone. He'd miss her smell and touch and questions about the coming day. What calf they'd wean? What field they'd put the cows in? He might be a father again by now; if not by now, then by morning – and eight cows to milk and pigs to feed and hens – he never had anything to do with the hens – maybe his mother, my granny would see to them. He stared at his old trousers and the crumpled shirt.

'What will become of us?'. He never had a thought like that before. The question only raised by his reluctance to change into his old gear. But the question stood. Three childer now and prices low. A house with little room and no bathroom. His mother who takes up a whole room, but has a pension. Where would we put a bathroom, even if we had one? That landing is the only room that's not a bedroom – apart from the kitchen, the scullery and the parlour – but you couldn't put a bathroom on the landing, could ya? His thoughts were straying and then, a cackling cry came from downstairs, my granny smelling procrastination.

"Hi Jim, you may bring these two out with ya... to do the things – I thought you'd have the cows in by now. That Red One is lookin'! Ya may keep her in when the milking's done. Did Pauline bring a proper nightdress to that hospital, if she wears the one she came down in the other morning, they'll send her home... with no baby – Do ya hear me?". "Aye... aye..." was his only response.

There are few things worse than the unnatural procedure of changing your clothes after coming back from church or town. Going from good clothes into farming garb. Bringing to an end your heightened state of immunity from work and misery. A backward step like no other, as if someone stole the butter from your bread. My father liked being in his suit, he was tall and liked being tall. He was thin and clothes hung on him well. He'd have made a great idle man, but his conscience, his circumstance and his bullish mother had turned him into a worker. He had duty and responsibility and the hungriest mouth yet to feed. But first the cows.

If you stood at the back door of our old house – you'd see to the right, a row of outhouses covered in one galvanized roof. The piggery; the byre; the stable; the barn. Beyond that, the hayshed and beyond that again, the henhouse. To the left, a shed for turf and a workshop. Beyond that the haggard, a three-cornered garden where a hay pike would sometimes be built and where old machinery lay. In between a cobbled street.

This was our farmyard, our concentration camp. This is where the Rourkes – with and without the 'O' – did the things. The pigs were fed – the cows milked – the milk, strained, spilt, warmed, chilled and spilt again, the cans were rattled and buckets kicked – the hens were fed, tried and counted – the eggs were carefully collected – the byre was cleaned out – the calves sucked – hay carried here there and everywhere –and if it was raining, we swept the street. These chores were sometimes a pleasure – sometimes – and sometimes like this evening, they seemed to take forever.

When the things were done and all in bed, including Granny, my father went to a rectangular tin box on the top of the kitchen cabinet. Because of his height, my father had a world of hidey places all to himself. On the tops of presses, shelves and dressers; above the stairs and behind the clock – places out of reach to anyone under six foot. I discovered them when I was fourteen. A treasure trove of knick-knacks and naughties – pen-knives, pens and razors. Pipes, poteen and in this colourful tin box, three John Player cigarettes. He wasn't a smoker, an occasional smoker at best, but tonight was a special night. He pulled a bristle from the twig and lit it with an amber from the range – he jump-started his fag – saved a match and went outside to gaze at the stars.

Micky McGerty asked me, the night of my father's wake *"Did he smoke much?"*. I said *"On and off"*. He said he remembered Daddy as a young fella arriving at the creamery one morning with a fag butt behind his ear – he asked Georgie Taylor for a light. Georgie was from Killashandra and very tight, but kind-hearted in a way and he gave the Auld Lad a match. There was a wind that morning coming in around Annagh hill. My father put the butt in his mouth and lit the match. The wind took it. He lit another and it did the same. Georgie was alarmed at his wastefulness and lack of technique. After the third match had quenched, Georgie snapped at my father, *"Are ya long smoking, Sonny?"*. My father's reply – *"I haven't started yet"*.

My father wasn't one for looking at the stars, that would be on a par with reading books and playing the fiddle, but he was going to smoke this one fag, look up into the sky and make a wish. He wished for a baby girl. Why? He was a gentle soul – he could relate to the female of the species with great ease. An understanding that was hard found in men of the time. He was a charmer – plus, the pressure of being a role model to two boys might be more that he could bear. They had talked about names – Geraldine, Sarah or Mary-Ann. Boys names hadn't been discussed as much, maybe James and maybe not.

He sucked and puffed at his fag. There's a satisfaction that comes when work is done. He embraced it. That's when he saw it – a strange moving light. The tiniest of dots. It came from down towards the road. It bobbed and moved and then gradually came to a halt. It was now at the foot of the lane between the two piers. It began to fade, then shot up and shone bright again. My father gathered himself, pulled a drag from his John Player – the hairs were straightening on the back of his neck... and then the penny dropped. It was a cigarette. Donald Murray was on his way home from a céilí up the road. He was a smoker, a proper smoker. The light my father could see was Donald's 'Sweet Afton'. It stopped because Donald had stopped and was looking up at my father's cigarette. Daddy called out and went to the road.

Donald Murray was six foot seven and stuck to the tar – questioning his own cowardice in the face of the unknown. They were both rattled and uncomfortable in their subsequent dialogue.

"You were up the road?"

"I was."

"How is McCaffery?"

"Pat's in bed."

"Is he sick?"

"I didn't ask."

"How's the other fella?"

"Oh now, telling lies."

Donald was much the same age as my father, he was a bachelor – he lived in Drumbrick, a quarter mile towards Drumeela Chapel. We called that road Bachelor's Road – we could have called any road near us by the same name. These men spent their evenings going a céilí – visiting – playing cards and telling lies. They communicated in lies and stories. Truth was hard to come by in those places – still is – and truth never sparkled like a good lie. And so, lies were a valued commodity. If you could tell a good one, you'd be welcome almost anywhere. But not in our house. My granny didn't tolerate these men. Their angst too recognisable – too close to the bone. When she moved out some months later, the door was always off the latch – they came then and they brought plenty.

My father always found it hard to extract conversation from Donald Murray and tonight, in light of these not very well explained, ghostly lights – he was even more restrained. Still my father tried:

"My woman is in Manorhamilton."

"Aye, what took her down there?"

"She went in to have a baby."

"Aye... (long silence) *Did your heifer calf?"*

"She did... "

"On her own?"

"Aye. (and then) *I'll let you go home, Donald, you won't find midnight."*

"Aye... and it was the fag, you say?"

"Aye... I'd say that's what it was... aye!"

"Aye..."

Donald moved on, not fully convinced, yet showing no sign of fear. But he was afraid, my father too. They knew the light had its source, but that's not what scared them. It was the moment when they both became aware of their own vulnerability.

CHAPTER 3

A Beautiful Baby Boy

My Father came stumbling out of the stable the following morning, a bucket in each hand. He was after feeding two suck calves. The stable had been vacated by the horse not long ago. The humble steed, sadly sold and replaced by a Ferguson 20 tractor. The stable was now home to the calves. The doorways into all these outhouses were low and uncomfortable for a tall man like my father. The calves this morning, more energetic than usual, dunting and driving him out the door – *"Go back"* – the Auld Lad destroyed with warm milk and shit and slobber, banged his head on the way out too – not so fond of being tall today. The cows roaring, the pigs squealing and Granny at the back door giving orders. It was ten past nine.

And it was Friday, it was cold and wet – haskey – the spring nowhere to be seen and no word from the hospital. Maybe later he would ring from Hyland's shop. For now though, his mother's voice ringing around the farmyard:

"Are the cows milked or what are they roarin' for?
You may let them out. Where are ya putting them?
You may feed that sow or she'll lose her voice. Did
ya put in the hens last night before ya went to bed.
There's a fox eyeing them up this good while. There
are several ones gone to the creamery already and
we've not a can in sight. That woman of yours must
have decided against having the baby."

Daddy let out the cows and brought them over the pass
towards Baxter's hill. He didn't have to bring them all
the way to the gardens at the top of Baxter's hill, but he
did. This morning, putting distance between himself
and his mother was satisfying and essential.

All our fields and meadows had names – usually
associated with their origin. Baxter's Hill never
belonged to the Baxters, but they lived there. The
remnants of their house still evident and the gardens
grown over. These nooks and crannies of the farm
fascinated my father – how did these people survive?
There was a big family of them, all got away and done
well. Daddy got away one time too – went to work on a
farm across the border in Teemore. It was only a half an
hour away, but it was away all the same. He worked and
lived with a Protestant family, they were decent and
kind and didn't have a granny, but he had to come
home, when his older brother, Michael, my uncle, went
to America.

From his vantage point, my father had a panoramic
view of three provinces – Connacht, Ulster and
Leinster. His eyes drawn well into the counties of

Fermanagh, Cavan, Longford and Leitrim. He could see the Sliabh an Iarainn mountains, Bruce mountain and Corriga hill. He could also see a shiny black car turning up our lane. It was Joey Hyland! He'd be bringing news from the hospital and the Auld Lad had to get back down to the house before Granny had the whole news got.

My father didn't run – ever – well if he did, I never saw him. But this morning, he sort of glided down the hill on the wind, his will taking him faster than his legs could carry him. He came around the corner of the house as calm as a turkey in June, as if just back from his morning stroll. Joey, not used to calling, drove up to the back street beside the haggard, my father met him there. This location was out of favour with Granny. She only accepted visitors on the front street, beside the front door, where they could notice the good wallpaper in the hall and the shiny door knob.

Joey brought a parcel for the day that was in it. In it, was fish for Friday, custard, jam and Jelly Tots. My sister and brother toddled down to see what was going on, encouraged by their granny, as they might relay news quicker than some. It was them that Joey addressed first:

"And you two sweethearts have a new baby brother – born yesterday evening at five past eight on the 11th of March 1965. A beautiful baby boy – seven pounds, eight ounces –Mother and baby doing well!"
He turned to my father.

"What do you think of that – Mr O'Rourke?"

My father stared at the parcel: *"Aye, well sure as long as everything went all right"*

My sister and brother begged the Auld Fella to open up the parcel, so that they could get a look at the new baby, my granny shouting *'Hello Joe'* from the back door. My father trying to put into words, his gratitude for the kindness shown by the Hylands and at the same time, hold back the enormous pride and love he had for his wife and soulmate who would soon be home and their lives would feel warm and complete again.

"What price is sweets", Granny asked. She was trying to work out the value of Hylands parcel. Its contents had been put away. The fish to the cold press in the scullery, the custard to the glass cabinet in the parlour, where the non-essentials were kept; the jam left in at the back of the everyday press and the sweets in the cubby hole above the stairs until lent was over. *"It's a pity he didn't bring the paper, it would have saved us going up today"*. My father was having his porridge before he brought our can of milk to the creamery. Margaret and Kevin hadn't started school yet, they were playing brothers and sisters under the table – a well-rounded turnip represented the new baby, my stand-in double. *"Don't let that baby fall, it has to do two dinners"*, Granny chewed. Thank God! – my granny had a sense of humour after all.

By the Way – I don't mean to make my granny out to be a monster. She wasn't. But I do need someone to be the villain, as there was a particular shortage of villains in these early days. So, like the turnip in my siblings' game, I need her to stand in – at least for now, but for the record – I was very fond of her. She could be lovely, but mostly, she was hard as nails, proud to a fault and in her later years, very fond of Bingo. She had spent some time in the States, that made her brassy. Having your nest taken over by a feisty young one. Well that just makes you mean.

Daddy shaved after the breakfast – a ritual that would not be rushed by fire or flood, even Granny accepted this arduous siege. His long thin face was washed and shaved like he was about to run off with a nun. Not a hair on his head would be left out of place. The calves can dunt and puck all they want, but my father's face will always be clean and smooth and smelling of soap and aftershave. He propped the twelve-gallon creamery can on the back of the tractor and headed off whistling down the road. This was his time. Off to the creamery on his own.

He headed over the Drumbrick road – Bachelor's road, past Donald Murray's house – to Drumeela Chapel where we went to Mass – past Kate Dolan's shop and post office where I learned to borrow and pay back another day – by O'Brien's pub and story factory – down by Drumeela National School where I would go, to learn, to play, to fight, to resist and eventually leave unscathed. After the school he turned right over by Annagh lane and on to Longfield and McGerty's shop, and bar. And there on the lower side of the road was the Creamery, where local farmers brought their milk and bought their feed and artificial manure and teat dip.

There was a formality here, that we as country folk respected and enjoyed. Men on tractors, cars with trailers; carts drawn by horses and one man with his milk churn balanced on his bike – all queued up and waited for their turn. Two men to a can, lifted and grabbed by two men on the platform, the can slid across a polished floor of milky blue. The lid loosened – two, three and lift – the milk poured into the funneled drum – quality checked and volume measured – empty can – lid back on... There was an excitement as your time came near, your chance to shine – this was where you became part of a team. You helped the man before you, as the next man would be helping you. My father was well got here. His arms were long and when his turn came, he could take the pressure of this well-rehearsed routine. Some bottled it, some got excited and danced a different dance, but not him.

Along with this, the men chatted and pranced and kept time. You needed quick wit and timing here. Daddy was at his best in these surroundings. The subjects varied – chit-chat when things were slow, but more often than not, Benny Reilly would be there or Edward Kiernan and they'd have a tall tale to tell about de Valera or Franco or Jim McCartin's mare. *"Wait till I tell ya about Jim McCartin's mare"*.

After their main performance, the men fell into clusters of their own choosing. Today my father found himself chatting with Sean Sutherland of Toome, an industrious man, although his father was a great fiddle player. He had taught my grandfather, but Sean's father could both fiddle *and* work. Sean was normally edgy and gone home by now, but not today. Today he was calm – a broad smile and mellow – very mellow. He seemed half drunk. He proclaimed to my father that he was now a Daddy:

> *"Herself had the baby – a girl – Ann – lovely baby – came home yesterday – not talking yet – fierce nice girl and her only the size of a hot-water-bottle. Isn't nature an amazing thing when you think about it... What about Pauline? She's due sometime soon too... I hope all goes well. It's a very strange... magical thing, to see them coming into a house."*

My father decided against squaring up to Sean's good news. Why should he dilute his joy? He congratulated him and concurred!

CHAPTER 4

Drumshangore

I was landed home to the house in Drumshangore. I lay on a wee sleeping tray that had been handed down from my brother. Anything I ever got from my brother was intact and well cared for – shoes; football boots; school books. The latter with little or no wear. I was a week home from the hospital and it was fierce warm. I was at the kitchen table, a place I've tended to gravitate towards all my life. I was on the floor, looking over at the Rayburn Range. On one side of the range there was a pen. In this pen there was a pet pig. A hungry creature and a desperate smell off him. Not far away in a wooden box were twelve Rhode-Island-Reds –chirping. These were day-old chicks who needed the bit of incubation and where better to get it, than in our kitchen? Mammy had two Aran cardigans knitted since she got home from the hospital. Mammy knitted for a woollen company in Donegal, a handy way to subsidize the farm. She usually knitted three garments a fortnight, but had only knitted two since me.

Our kitchen was the hub of our lives – if the farm was our solar system – then the kitchen was our mission control. If you stood with your back to the range, you had a very red backside and a door on your immediate right. This was the spare room where Granny slept. She slept in other places too, very prone to nodding off, but this was where she went at night. On the right wall was the door to the scullery and access to the back door and farmyard. In front to the right were the stairs, closed in with a flimsy door at the foot. On the left wall was a window that looked out to the front of the house and the lane and the road. Back left was the door to the front hall which led to the front door and to the parlour. The parlour had good carpet, good wallpaper and nice things, but we only went in there for the custard or when Santy'd come, or the priest – all roughly once a year.

The kitchen table was by the window – Daddy sat at the head, under the clock. Mammy seldom sat – a bee in her bottom, driven to please and to serve. Granny grinded at the other end. The rest of us sat where we could and ate lots – always. When Mammy brought me back from the hospital, the house was tidy. Granny had gone mad sweeping, clearing and tidying, so as to make a point. Any extra clutter was fired into the spare room, her room – most of it her stuff in the first place, and the house was cleaned and polished. *"A lovely house to come back to"*, my mother said. She didn't mean a bit of it. Never was a cold war carried out in such complementary tones.

Mammy was from Druminchingore, hardly a mile down the road towards Newtown. She was an only child. Her mother died when she was a year and eight months. Her father, John Maguire wasn't able or expected to look after a small baby and so my mother was sent to Arvagh, County Cavan to be minded and reared by her Aunt Mary-Kate. Her father John kept in contact and would cycle the ten miles to Arvagh every week without fail, until she returned home in 1955, when she was thirteen. My mother has nothing but sweet-scented anecdotes from her time in the county Cavan. Her side always had the eyes hopping out of their heads with villainy and devilment, dissolving any sense of foreboding with a tap on the elbow and a good yarn. She had a charmed life in some ways, lavished with kindness by her cousins and her loving aunts and uncles – protected, but never pitied – prompted, but never pushed – surrounded, yet still an only child. She got 'some land' when she came back to Druminchin – she got an even bigger land when she married Jim Rourke and moved in with his mother.

Granny was great at minding childer. Her empathy was low and her resistance to crying and snarling was fantastic. She could out-snarl any snarling child and make them tired, very tired. We were all tired when Granny was minding us – slept like babies – some of us were babies. The whole idea in Granny minding us, was that my mother could get back out on the farm as quickly as possible – she was the right height for darting in and out of those tiny doorways that had been so troublesome while she was away. The cows were milked by hand – she'd milk two for Daddy's one. She fed and de-horned the calves, cleaned out the byre and looked after the hens. The knitting could be done at night.

Because I was only the week home, I was parked, most of the time, on the floor on this tray – in between Granny's legs – a drafty enough spot in a very warm kitchen. The view was diverse. I could either look towards the range and the pigs and the fowl, or I could look behind me, deep into the canyon of Granny's thighs. Rockface made up of tights and bloomers and hay-ropes. There was wild-life there too, buffalo and bears and small birds – the odd rip of thunder and sometimes, like tumbleweed, a mothball would roll by. She slept after meals or when she didn't want to hear, but she looked after us well – kept us away from the fire and the Big Knife and taught us our prayers.

The hens were her idea. When she came to Drumshangore in 1920 she was twenty-four – her husband was thirty-eight. There were only a few cows and pigs and far too much fiddling. She started to keep hens and sell eggs in order to prop up the income. Hens are easy, if you can keep the fox away. They had a base at the henhouse, but wandered about the farmyard and pecked and nodded and examined. They have small brains or so they say, but what brains would you want if you were a hen. It was often considered a flaw, down our way – to have too much brains – *"That man is a fool, he has too much brains"*. No – better be like a hen – and nod and peck.

The pig was an orphan; a bit like Mammy when her mother died. For the pig, having to stay in our kitchen was the equivalent of Mammy having to go and stay in Arvagh. And like her, the pet pig was always well looked after. The makings of a valued animal. Of course, back then, apart from the odd kickidy cow, the animals were all pets – rubbed and patted and hugged, a damn sight more than we were. Childer are a nuisance on a farm until they get to three or four and can stand in gaps and hold wool and sweep the street. Margaret was four at that time and was in charge of washing dishes; going to the well; finding radio Luxembourg; filling the tank and emptying the pots. Kevin was two and a half and when he wasn't doing chin-ups in the shed, was chopping sticks and learning to drive. All I could do was nod.

On the side of the Rayburn, there was a water tank. The tank was filled with water from a barrel at the back of the house. This was water that had been collected from the roof via the gutters and downpipe. Rainwater. A softer water than you'd get in the well. We used this water when it got warmed up by the range, for washing ourselves. We used this water sparingly, because no one liked filling the tank. Our hearts sinking when the Auld Lad would go for a big wash. The scullery door closed over and for the next twenty minutes, ploshing and scrubbing and Mammy carrying the hot water to him. And then – *"Some of yez, go and fill up that tank"*.

Mammy was much smaller and didn't have to wash as much. Granny never seemed to wash – just stuck another moth ball down her drawers. On Saturday night, a tin bathtub was brought in from the barn and we were savagely attacked by our mother with cloths and Brillo pads and bogging her fingers into our ears and scolding us in the rinse. There's a lot to be said for moth balls down your pants.

While Granny was in our house, God was everywhere. We got constant reminders of his whereabouts and his mood. You could do nothing without him appearing around the corner, he was mostly sad and disappointed. Sticking your finger in the sugar bowl was one of the biggest sins, up there with licking the lid off the jam jar, but not as bad as *not* filling the tank. Not only was that a sin; but you would also be responsible for the cooker exploding and the whole house going up in smoke.

In the evenings, we thanked God for his intrusiveness and sorrowful disposition by saying the rosary. This was a long, drawn out, somber event and I often wondered about its validity. Everyone taking up half positions of prayer. No one committing fully to the cause. Daddy on one knee, Mammy on two... but knitting. I was watching – Granny was using up all the oxygen, and the other two – suffocating with the sudden loss in cabin pressure.

I lay there staring at the pig, the chickens and the fullest side tank in all of South Leitrim. I took this to be my norm. Another tumbleweed rolled by – in the distance, a thunder storm. I got a sense of three generations, all of different thinking – the same hymn sheet, yet different singing. All together, yet each to their own. Normal, yet slightly off and to one side. I was only at the beginning – I was only the size of a small bed – how was I to know what lay ahead – I thought someone else would sort that out – if not, the prayer would kick in and make everything all right.

The kettle was boiling now. The kettle was always boiling in our house – it still does. The clock was ticking – it would continue, although we never went hard on time. Granny mentioned a saint; everyone said *"Pray for us..."* We can only assume that they did. Mammy said *"Knit one purl one"*. Week one – done. More still to come.

CHAPTER 5

Chaos in the Church

Jim Rourke was shaving again. It was Sunday – he had skipped shaving on Saturday, so that he would have a little more growth on Sunday and thus give him more grip with the razor. Today was my christening – in Drumeela. The car was back from Brewster's garage – washed and going with a hum. Granny was washed too – a horrendous ordeal that took place the previous evening. While the Auld Pair were out doing the things, she took into it right before my very eyes. It wasn't pretty – bars of soap were lost as folds of flesh were swept aside. Some small animals ran for cover and some stayed – stuck their noses out and yawned. She was now in her American fur coat and hat – heading over to Mass. She sat in front of the black Ford Anglia with her son at the wheel. Mammy was in the back, wiping everyone's faces with a glove that she kept in her prayer book.

The crowds at the church stood back as we arrived, thinking it was the Soviet Union's new Head of State coming to Drumeela Mass – because that's who my grandmother – soon to be my Godmother – looked like... a Russian Leader in her fur coat and hat. She played the part to a tee. She walked up the steps like royalty. Meanwhile, Mammy and Daddy were playing pass-the-parcel with me at the car. Mam had crocheted me a Baptismal gown that'd fit Donald Murray. It was all holes, catching my toes and fingers. Only for the day that was in it, I might have complained, but no, I went with the flow. Margaret was dressed up in some lovely homemade gear too and Kevin got the short straw – a miniature suit that came in a parcel from the States. *"We're a right looking crowd"*, my mother said – she's said that many's the time since.

Because of the christening, we had to march up to the front. Granny loved that. Christy Mimna hopped into the seat beside her when she got parked. *"Hello Auntie Maggie"*, he whispered – that didn't go down well and she took out her prayer beads and started to pray like billyo.

So, this was Drumeela chapel. This was my first visit. I was impressed. Who wouldn't be? A place where you left your weekly drudge at the door and sat and kneeled and stood and murmured and sang. None of it of your own initiative – just do what the lad beside you is doing – or the lad up top.

The lad up top was Father Lynch. Father Lynch gave my mother a clatter once for dancing with my dad – from what I recall of their dancing it was the Auld Lad he should have hit – but the story goes:

Mammy snuck into a dance in Carrigallen hall when she was seventeen – she was just about to marry my father, so she needed at least one slither around the boards with him before she did. They danced their 'Where will I leave down this wet bag of cement' – dance and might even have enjoyed themselves. Father Lynch was at the back of the hall watching. When my mother went to a 'Pioneer' meeting, some days later the priest asked her to stay on after the meeting – he wanted to have a word with her. In this private meeting, he told her he had seen her at the dance; that she was only seventeen; that Jim Rourke was thirty-two and that somewhere in there, a major rule had been broken. He was disappointed and saddened and finished the conversation by giving her a good clatter across the back of the head. She didn't cry or give the hoor any satisfaction and went home. A year later Father Lynch concelebrated Mass at her wedding. That day, Father Lynch was as nice as pie and ate pie, loads of pie and a big feed of roast beef and spuds and anything that was going. My mother didn't want him there, let alone be above on the alter. But Granny and Father Lynch were very 'great' and that was it. No more to be said.

Still, I liked this tiny church. It was modest and welcoming and the people who went there were kind and kind of mad and not too caught up in the kneeling and the murmuring and the bowing. Ten o'clock Mass in Drumeela was a must; a carnival of normality; a catwalk of calamity; and outside afterwards, the biggest open-air asylum in South Leitrim. Everyone sat at the back of the tiny church and the back was always packed. Those who came in late had to sit at the front. The men's side was the Drumbrick side, the women were on the Drumeela side. John McCarron, who fought in some war or other and had post-traumatic-stress-disorder – he sat on his own somewhere and often blurted out during Mass – *"Come out ya bastards"; "Holly Mary, full of God"; "God save us from the Devil"*. The choir were always slightly off – too busy singing to hear the note. The altar boys fought over the ringing of the bell, the boys at the back fought over the current belle – 'The Belle of Drumeela' as she headed to the alter – their adoration finely balanced on her hips. Shafts of light cut the eyes out of hung-over heads and old ladies in their scarves prayed for vocations.

Here we'd gather when all was well. Here we'd gather when all else failed. Here we'd pray for rain or hay weather or our local football team. Here's where we'd celebrate Christmas and St Patrick and Jesus dying on the cross and here we'd sympathize and say *"Sorry for your loss"*. I would say goodbye to Granny here and my father too and some I hardly knew. Sometimes I'd be sent, because that'd be a funeral for us. And here, sometimes, I would be crippled with pain and loss and no one knew – because I was no relation of the deceased and only relations back then were allowed to grieve or cry and bear their cross.

I studied Granny as we sat up at the top end of the church – a proud Godmother – She loved anything with God in it. She was a religious woman; genuinely believed and was trying very hard to be as good as she could be. She didn't like to fail, but didn't wilt when failure came. She was proud even when the word was used against her. She took responsibility for her actions – decisions she made when clouded in paranoia or when crystal clear in thought. She was big and demanded big, but she also had her secrets and she had her doubts and she had her doubts about me right from the start. She knew I wasn't to be trusted. Call it intuition, but she knew that I noticed things and that it might come back to bite her – she didn't know how or when or where... but she knew by the look of my pudgy face and the glint in my roguish eye, that I was always up to something and she was right. Even that morning, when I should have been concentrating on my prayers, I noticed something that I knew could get messy, but I didn't say a word – I just let it happen. I was an awful two-week-old child. And although this episode is more to do with physics and mechanics, it is also to do with vanity and neglect and prayer and a hole in granny's coat.

Because it was my day – and let's face it, it was my christening - Granny took ownership of me – I was centre stage and if she was holding me, then so was she. I don't have a problem with that – I'd be the same myself. But Granny also had to take out the rosary beads – as much for show as anything else – and when she was pretend praying on the beads, they got caught in a loose thread of the crocheted gown which Mammy didn't have time to fully finish – between the milking and the hens and the knitting – she just didn't have time to tie up the loose ends – and now it was entangled in Granny's beads. When it came near the time for dousing me with the holy water, granny shoved her beads into her fur coat pocket – but the pocket of the fur coat had a hole in it and the beads – now connected to the gown by a ravelling thread – fell through the hole and onto the floor and when they fell to the floor, Christy Mimna picked them up and handed them back to granny and said – *"Here's your beads, Aunty Maggie"*. Granny snapped them back and shoved them into her pocket, again, with the same result. All the time the thread of my gown was being anchored onto Granny's coat. What could go wrong says you? It was then time for Granny to hand me over to the priest. She got up out of the seat and stepped into the aisle – all lipstick and smiles and handed me over to her good friend Father Lynch. As he took me, Granny's beads fell out of her pocket once more and this time she bent down to grab them – as she did – Father Lynch took off with me to the Holy Water font on the alter. My trailing thread was still attached to the coat and we pulled the tail of Granny's coat over her head.

It's here we bring up the phrase – all fur coat and no knickers – because although Granny had all the furry animals well fenced in, with tights and bloomers and hay rope – she had little else in the way of a frock or dress or even a dishcloth to cover her rather large and imposing rear end. Country women back then spent little time on what was under the coat – as long as they had a good coat – and Granny had a great one – a fierce heavy fur coat from America and she used to get very warm when she wore it; the less you wore under it the better. You'd never expect to be exposing yourself above at the altar of Drumeela Chapel.

As the fresh air hit Granny's backside – she sprang from her position like an Olympic gymnast and with great speed and agility – she snipped the tightening thread with her dagger like dentures; released the tail of her coat and gently slid back into the seat beside my now godfather, Christy Mimna. The priest proceeded unaware and I said to myself, *"Fair play to Granny – she can move when she wants to"*. The congregation craned and whispered and I was baptized unnoticed. I was already a ravelling Catholic.

For a huge part of my life, religion played a huge part in it. It filled in all the gaps, smoothed over the cracks and gave cause for celebration and sweets. We swayed over and back to Drumeela in a rhythm that gave comfort and solace without demanding too much of our commitment. Yes, we had to do the things early on a Sunday – yes, we had to clean ourselves and dress up a bit – even Granny started to wear clothes under her Mass coat – and there was also a little guilt attached here and there, but in general, religion was easy and unquestioned.

CHAPTER 6

The Early Harvester

Everyone was sleeping. The moon shone through the window where we emptied the pots. I was now upstairs in a room with my brother. Kevin slept in the bed – I was in the cot. There was a huge picture of St Patrick hanging on a partition wall which separated our room from our sister's. St Patrick had a load of snakes at his feet and was staring down at me and my brother. My mother later told us, that the snakes represented the scattered clothes on our bedroom floor and that St Patrick was telling us to tidy our room. We never fell for it. We continued to have snakes in that room right up until we moved into the new house in 1983.

There was a wardrobe and a bed and two doors – one leading onto the landing and the other through the partition. That would become known as the Girls' Room. For seventeen years, my sisters, one and two would go through our room to get to theirs – never knocking, never saying sorry to intrude – only stopping every once in a while, to say how untidy we were or asking what was the smell? The smell was none of their business – it was usually my business... in the pot under the bed. In the main, we were segregated and civil – like this morning – all there was was a very cute baby waiting patiently for something to happen.

I was three months old now. It was July and somewhere near dawn. I had been awake for a while, but didn't cry or move. I wasn't scared – just looking about me – someone had done a very good job on the wallpaper. That would be Mammy – she was an expert. It wasn't nice wallpaper – a roll of seconds out of 'Keiths' – just that the joints were so well matched. She had great patience for the like of that. The three-foot by foot-and-a-half wooden sash window sometimes whistled and sometimes rattled, but not this morning. Now, there was nothing but gnawing. A mouse somewhere was hard at work – continuing the secret passageways through the house. This was a well thought of mouse – keeping his head down and getting on with it – not like the auld fashioned mice that sometimes walked into the kitchen and strutted about like they owned the place. Those mice were despised by my father and mother. *"Would ya look at that fella and the brazen head on him"* and then, whatever was in their hand – apart from a cup or a bit of bread – they'd fire at the hoor – a turf, the Leitrim Observer, the Anglo Celt, the poker. There was no place in our house for mice that got above their station. We had a three-legged cat at the time, who, because of his disability, wasn't expected or encouraged to run after mice. And there was me, who hadn't started walking yet – thinking a third leg might be useful.

This nibbling mouse continued and his timing sparked the morning's rise. I heard the slightest chirp outside, then a rustle in a bush, another chirp and then a squawk, and slowly and relentlessly the world around me began to wake. Along with the birdsong and the mice – I heard whispers from my parents' room. My father was making moves and so was my mother – there was work to be done. They had carefully put this day aside for mowing and there wasn't a minute to lose.

The forecast had said there was a good spell coming. The talk at Mass and the creamery was of hay weather. The coming few days were crucial. The Auld Fella had stayed late in the shed the night before, sharpening a blade and replacing sections. The mowing arm was taken from the Haggard, greased, limbered and put on the back of the tractor. My father was ready – the machinery was ready. Mowing with the tractor was still a novelty, as was getting up at first light. A man who got up at this time, didn't have to do much else to make a triumph of his day. The three small meadows would be mowed before the milking. I let out a squeal, just in case they went off without me.

Our door to the landing had no lock nor handle. It was closed over to keep out the light in summer - otherwise it had no real function. The icy draughts in winter would freeze you – door or no door. This morning it opened softly and Mammy came in. Her look of *'Ya little buck ya'*, was already familiar. A playful lament, as I must have been shocking cute at the time. She swept me up into her arms, admired me, changed me, dressed me, wrapped me in several blankets and put me into a basket with a bottle. I hadn't even time to say, *"What's happening this morning, Mam?"*. I was brought outside and put sitting on the street while Mammy and Daddy went from outhouse to outhouse looking for the 'bloody' rake. Eventually the tools were found – the Auld Lad mounted the tractor like a cowboy getting up on his horse and we were off.

He drove down the lane and turned in at the field under the road, Mammy followed with me and a rake and a pitchfork. There was a mist down towards Clogher Cross. Although it was bright, there was no sun yet. The tractor reached Grimes' meadow – a two-acre plot of ground which we had got from 'The Land Commission'. A welcome addition to the farm, even if the soil was poor. The Auld Fella let down the arm of the mower – looked to the skies and then to Mammy for reassurance. She was always ready for the fight.

I was planked near the gap in case I'd be forgot about and then my parents, without fuss or conversation set about mowing the first of the year. It was half four in the morning. The other two would wake in their own time and run down to Granny – I was as snug as a bug in a rug and the weather was up – or so we hoped. My father did a couple of rounds with the mower and my mother raked out the backing swarth. The crop was light and there were no hiccups. They still had to do the things and the creamery and the never-ending cycle of jobs, but this morning – here together as the sun finally rose over Baxter's hill – they were as happy and as content as they'd ever be. The 'Twenty' slowly purred along and my father, like he was astride a huge combine-harvester in a fifty-acre field of corn, carefully guided his machine and whistled 'The Rocks of Bawn'.

There's a card game played locally called 'Twenty-Five'. This game is simple and straightforward and like most card games, depends on the hand you are dealt. Some men could play a bad hand well and others make a good hand look poor. Some farmers near us, who had fine farms, crowed about them lots and made little of them. My father and mother were not dealt a good hand when it came to farming, but they hoaked and poked and gnawed at the shallow soil... played their hand as best they could and somehow stayed in the game.

They never buckled at the sight of work. They never envied what others had. They just got up in the morning, put on their clothes and began. They didn't strike oil or gold – but in some ways this was their gold – a whole way of life – simple and straightforward and cautiously played. That was the part of Twenty-Five that I despised. There was so much caution and waiting and holding on.

When I started playing this card game first– I was often reprimanded for 'stuffing' – throwing in my good card when there were still men to play. It wasn't against the rules – just reckless and unsure. But I didn't want to wait. No youngster wants to wait. My worst nightmare is to be on my deathbed, gasping my last breath and realising that I still have the five of trump or the ace of hearts in my fist.

When Grimes' Meadow was mowed, the arm of the mower was put upright for the short journey down to the cross. At Clogher Cross we had two meadows, one either side of the road. One, nothing more than a triangular quarter acre, that took as much time to mow as a decent bit of ground. The other was important to the farm and the community in equal measure. It was a flat rectangular field that stretched along the river. Each year when the hay was won and gathered this became the football field. It's only about half the size of a proper football pitch, but it was flat and available and along the road. My father, although not a footballer himself, was a football fanatic and knew the importance of this venue and so got double pleasure when it came time to mow.

By half eight, the three meadows were cut and the three of us were sitting in at the table having our breakfast – the early breakfast. Porridge, tea and a cut of bread. Then it would be time for milking and doing the things. There was a swagger to my Auld Pair that morning, because the hay was down and the sun was trump.

I'm not a farmer – never was - I've never had any aspirations towards being a farmer. It never bothered me, I didn't reject it, it just wasn't my thing. Yet the countryside and it's sights and sounds and smells are indelibly ingrained in my make-up. There is nothing more comforting than the sound of birdsong or the hum of a tractor mowing in the distance. To see these Leitrim drumlins – our modest fields and meadows – carefully minded and played in. I'm often away now, but as I make my return, there is nothing more reassuring than the waft of freshly cut grass or the smell of a blossoming whin. Even a blast of slurry does it for me. It's just part of who I am.

CHAPTER 7

Minding Me

Mammy sat on a low wooden four-legged stool under the hard-milked cow. She leaned her head against the cow's side for traction and with a tit in each hand, she pulled and squeezed and made a rhythmic sound. This was the hardest played instrument on our farm. We had eight cows. The Red One; The Blue One; The Black One; The Black Heifer; The Kickidy One; The Big Cow; Fitz's Cow and last and by no means least – The Hard-Milked One. This was a good-natured animal, placid and obedient. No kicking or swinging a tail when you'd least expect it. But whatever way her tits were – she was almost impossible to milk. Daddy couldn't make any fist of her – did nothing but scold if he was asked to milk her. Then he just got angry or pretend angry, which amount to the same thing and then he'd huff. So, she was left for Mammy to strig. The only thing was, she didn't have –

just a strig! She was the best milker in the place, the most milk by a long shot. And so, for years Mammy gritted her teeth, sat in and found the rhythm. I was left to be minded by others.

I wasn't hard minded. I was always pudgy and slow. A bit docile you could say, but I knew the way I was and was happy there. I was in the cot most of the time or the pram when the work was outside. I was never held or petted – none of us were. Childer back then were fed and cleaned and left somewhere where an eye could be kept on them. The work had to go on. After a week with Mammy – the first week after I was born – I could tell I wasn't going to fly first class for long. I was quickly put in the care of Granny – she looked after me when I was inside. When I was outside, which was quite a lot of the time, I was put within ear-shot of my mother, but in the care of my older sister and brother – and boy did they look after me.

Margaret used to push me and the pram down the lane at high speed and then let go – taking bets from her other brother as to which hedge I'd end up in. A lot of experiments were carried out on me during that time. I forgive Kevin everything in this regard. Kevin never had a bad thought in his head – (Burstin' Drumreillys by the way is not a bad thought) – but Margaret was the ringleader. How far could they stretch me? How high could they bounce me? And how long could they hold my breath? Because when I eventually did cry, it was her job to hold her hand over my mouth in case Mammy heard the racket.

I was blessed to have such vigilant carers. Not once did my mother ever hear me cry. Even when I was made put my willy into a bottle of some unidentified substance – and it burned my 'lad' into a bright red blister.

It was my sister's job to go to the well. The well was not that far away in Gortaheeran – down the back lane, across the road into Micky Mac's meadow, along the pass, into McCabe's meadow and there it was. Only ten minutes away – for an adult. For a four-year-old, it was more like a half a day – a trail of death – through the farmyard and the pigs and the hens; across the public road; into a meadow owned by a mad man; across gates and fences and a narrow river – and you were there. What could go wrong? The well itself was a small pond. In spring it had loads of frogspawn. Margaret would be sent with two small buckets to get the water for drinking and making tea. When Kevin was out of the pram and able to tag along unaided, she put the buckets in the pram and used it as a cart. Now that I was around, the pram was back in vogue as a people carrier – But if I was put sideways and squished up to the front; there was still place for the two buckets – and if anything, they were a lot more stable.

Although some of these stunts were precarious and foolhardy – for me, there was a certain pleasure at being centre-stage. If I cried too often, I would be left in a heap at Granny's feet looking into the abyss. No – this was better and probably the most adventure I'd have for a while.

We were just lucky that no one fell into the river. Mind you – Micky Mac fell into a drain one time and the Auld Pair laughed for a week. We never thought of tragedy or worst-case scenarios – we just mucked and ducked about. I got stuck with a pitch-fork once – taking in hay. The Auld Lad bogged it into my leg, just under my backside. It was about three inches deep, but the fork was well worn and pointy and the prod didn't need a doctor. Instead I was put in a poultice – a heel off a pan loaf put over the cut to draw out the pus and badness, which I was told I had plenty of. This was strapped on with a tea towel and I was centre of attention for a day or two. I sat on an axe once too. I can't recount or even make up what I was doing at the time – maybe just looking for centre stage again. The scar is still there – four inches long – it's on the left cheek of my arse, if you're ever passing. It too required a poultice and sleeping on my front.

My mother had taken a bucket of milk from the hard-milked cow. There was always a second. Daddy had eaten his porridge and shaved; Granny was catching flies. We stood by the tractor – well Margaret and Kevin stood – I was in the pram. We were waiting to wave goodbye to Daddy when he'd head off for the creamery. The other pair were giddy, Mammy feeling under pressure, trying to take the last drop from the cow.

Big Jim, as some called our father appeared at the back door. Washed, shaved, hair combed and smelling of 'Old Spice'. He put on his cap and like an astronaut from Apollo 1 he walked towards his rocket – the

Ferguson Twenty. He checked that it had its seat cushion – a manure bag with just the right amount of hay - Check! – Lift the bonnet and check for diesel - Check! Check the rear, make sure the drawbar is on, and the wooden platform which he had made up to carry the two cans - Check! We had two cans now, because it was summer and the peak of the milking season. The launch of Apollo 1 was now ready – apart from the fact that we were still waiting on Mammy to finish off the hard-milked cow. Astronaut O'Rourke placed one can on the Apollo vessel and when the Auld Lassie finally finished, she strained the milk into the last can – lid on – up on the yoke – a short rope was tied around the two cans and then – time for lift off.

Because of his height, my father had a unique way of getting up on the tractor. He'd sit up side-saddle first – then, with the elegance of a ballerina, swing his inside leg over the steering wheel to the other side. An action we loved and admired till the day our 'Twenty' was given up to progress.

Time to start the engine. Fuel on. A bit of throttle. The 'Twenty' didn't start on a key, oh no. Put in the choke – the choke was pulled out to stop the tractor – it had to be in to start it. Then, there was a button on the crank case above the break, you pushed that in with the side of your leg and tentatively pushed the gear lever towards 'start'. Then the cranking and turning and whining would begin – and that was just the Auld Lad! Eventually that old grey mule would cough and splutter into life. The engine would roar, blue smoke would climb out from the exhaust pipe and the Drumshangore Apollo was Go, Go, Go.

There was usually some pretend pushing and tomfoolery taking place at the back. My sister and brother giving their father a badly needed push off down the lane. *"Step back, will yez"*, my father would gently say. But not today. Today Margaret and Kevin stood silent and smiling either side of me in the pram – like 'The Railway Children' or a final scene from 'The Little House on the Prairie' – innocent; almost angelic – too angelic. The Auld Fella held up his farewell hand, put the tractor in gear and away - headed off down the lane – and me after him – in the pram. I was attached to Apollo 1. A rope had been tied to the front of the pram by my sister and when no one was looking, the red-haired damsel attached the other end to the drawbar of the tractor.

There was no panic, no one but my brother and sister could see what was going on. My father couldn't see, because he never looked back – once he got clearance for the creamery, that was him – gone – into another world. The noise of the engine meant he couldn't hear any cries, if there was any, but there wasn't any, not yet. I was quite happy – going a bit quicker than usual, but so far, so good. Mammy was gone off doing her chores – far too busy for this sort of carry-on. Margaret and Kevin started out thinking it was great craic, but their joy was gradually turning to trepidation. I was feeling less gleeful too as the pram started hopping about on the lane like a turkey on hot coals. The prams back then were well made, well sprung pieces of machinery and I was in mid-air most of the time.

And then the perambulator did one last buck-lep into the Leitrim sky – it landed on its side – skidding and sliding and knocking sparks from the wheels. My father had to stop at the end of the lane; the bread van was going by. The driver waving frantically at him. The Auld Lad waved back – a big surprised head on him – wondering how did the man driving the bread van know him. He might be one of the Blakes, my father thought. I was in the hedge by this. My sister came flying down the lane and was trying to untie the rope. My Father, for a moment, lost in thought. She untied me – he took off – and never noticed. I was shaken – not stirred. Never got a hug or nothing. My sister had enough to be doing – minding us!

CHAPTER 8

Daughty Moore

Daughty Moore lived in a tiny brick cottage, beside Clogher Cross. It was a ten-minute walk from our house. This side of Daughty's on the right, beside Clogher River, there was another water well – Clogher Well. My sister Margaret had heard about this well and she had heard about Daughty – a strange raggedy old witch who lived with a cat and fourteen pet mice. She had a nose like a half opened pen-knife and could whistle through her nostrils. She was the daughter of a pirate and was vicious and mean... so McCaffery said.

McCaffery was Eugene McCaffery who lived up the road towards Drumreilly. He and his brother Pat were our nearest neighbours. Eugene was outgoing and went to town and drank and visited anyone who would have him. He'd tell lies that'd walk to Mohill and back. His brother was more introvert and quiet. He was better got than Eugene. At least you could have a conversation with Pat, but Pat stayed at home. Their house was a three roomed cottage, with no light or electricity. The main room had an open fire, but the chimney was blocked. When the fire was on, the door was left open to let out the smoke and let in the light. At night, it would be closed to keep out the cold and the dark. There was a mud floor, uneven and worn with a 'forrom' on one side of the fire. This forrom was three foot long. It had two legs on one side and no legs on the other. You sat at a slant. The other side of the fire was a chair with three legs and propped up by newspapers. The two men looked like coal miners, just home from a shift.

These two boyos lived in exceptional conditions, but not because of poverty – they just decided against house-work and maintenance. A lot of bachelors at the time, and especially bachelor brothers chose this way, and some lived like kings. We never judged.

McCaffery had my sister drove demented about Daughty Moore – said she used to spit and eat childer. Mammy said not to mind McCaffery; that he was only an auld knave, but we had no business annoying that poor woman. The next time we were sent to the well Margaret decided to go to Clogher Well instead of Gortaheeran and check out this witch theory. We set off – me scrunched sideways in the front of the pram – the two buckets at the rear. Kevin ran on in front, cheering with excitement. At Clogher Cross, they turned for Carrigallen and went up the slight hill to the well. This was a proper watering hole with steps down to it and a wee concrete house built around it. No spawn or tadpoles or cow dung, just clear water. The buckets were filled and placed back in the pram with me and then there was a lot of whispering.

My big sister and brother decided it was time to call on Daughty Moore. If she did eat children, she'd love me, because I was a great big plump child and probably wouldn't even cry when she'd take a bite out of me. The plan was that they'd leave the pram at the door – knock – and then hide in the bushes and see what happened. If she ate me, she was a witch – if she didn't – well, it was back to the same dull existence of every other day.

When we got to Daughty's house, there was another conference with my siblings – they were deciding whether to leave the two buckets of water in the pram. It was one thing for the witch to eat the child, but what if she drank the two buckets of water – Mammy would kill them. They decided to take out the buckets of water and leave them at the road.

Then I was tidied up and made presentable. The snot was wiped from my nose as no witch would go for that. They pushed me to the door – said good-bye and were just about to retreat, when Daughty came around the corner of the house. They froze. And then with the warmth of an old aunt or a nice granny, she said *"This must be the Rourkes – come in till I give yez a biscuit"*. Margaret walloped Kevin for saying, *"No thanks"*. And we went into Daughty Moore's for our first afternoon tea.

Daughty was a refined little woman, originally from the North of Ireland. She had hints of grandeur still hanging on in her accent. The other two got orange and two biscuits each, I got poked at and prodded, but she never even took a bite out of me. It turns out she wasn't a witch at all. Fond of men is all she was. My mother told me years later, that she had a lot of boyfriends – the Egg Man was her favourite.

When we were leaving, Daughty said to call again anytime we were at the well. The other pair were in fierce humour the whole way home – went clean mad with the high intake of sugar. When we got back, Margaret had a big story for Granny. Granny looked at me in the pram – drier than usual after a trip to the well. Then Granny said, *"Where is the water?"*. The silly eegits forgot to put the buckets back in after the orange and biscuits. I was delighted, good enough for them and their bellies full. I stayed with Granny while they headed back to the well – walking and no pram.

Granny was getting fat. I only really noticed after I met Daughty Moore. Daughty was much the same age as Granny, but slight and petite and no big buggages of fat, like what Granny had. I had seen Granny togging out and it was plain to see she had let herself go. Was there some underlying problem? Well, apparently there was and it was me, or at least partly me. I was only five months old and had already caused the deterioration of my grandmother's health. Her physical and mental wellbeing were being jeopardised because I was slow at walking and talking and taking orders. She had enough of looking after me and the others and my mother had now, unknowingly, taken the upper hand in the cold war. She was too fit and able of an opponent to be going toe to toe with and Granny felt surplus to requirements. In her despair, she started eating ginger nut biscuits. When Hackett's travelling shop would come of a Saturday, Granny would go out first and buy seven packets of ginger nut biscuits. Mick Hackett would put them in a brown paper bag. She'd pay him and give him money towards the rest of the shopping – come back in and say, *"That's done now"*, and then Daddy would go out for the rest of the groceries and a chat with Mick Hackett.

No one knew that Granny was comfort eating – I'd get hit the odd time with a few crumbs when I'd be sitting between her legs, but for the most part, she nibbled away without anyone knowing. We thought she was just chewing her cud. She probably wasn't even aware herself – her body and mind compensating for something that was lacking. Once she was head of this household – one of the many women who were better than their husbands in every department apart from maybe telling a story and selling pigs. Better in the meadow and the bog, on the headland or in the bottom field, with the cows or making bread – these women drove from the front and without acclaim or bravado, they navigated and steered and rowed the boat. And now all there was, was ginger nuts.

One cool September evening, Daddy was listening to the radio – an All-Ireland hurling final was being broadcast from Dublin and it was his job to tune in. The women's job was to keep childer quiet. My granny went for a walk. It wasn't like her – not being one for idle time. But it was Sunday; the dinner was got early on account of the game; the house tidied and Pauline free to mind us. Margaret was starting school the next day.

Granny went outside to look at the flowers – the roses and dahlias and chrysanthemums. She thought she'd walk down the lane. The hedges were trimmed and neatly kept. She was proud of that – and the ornate gates at the road – not many had gates like them. Her eyes glanced to the field below the road, where the cows were. They were content as always. She kept walking, nothing to draw her back this evening it seemed. The brambles and the blackthorns lined both sides of the road towards Clogher Cross, the colours would be changing soon. She would be seventy soon – seventy was a good age back then, but Granny wanted more. At the cross she met Frank Mac; Frank was Micky's brother, he used to come up and sit at Clogher of a Sunday. Often the cross would be alive with young ones playing football and mixing through other, but not today. Granny didn't like Frank Mac or where he sat, she walked on towards the well. Just before the well there's a bridge where Clogher River runs under the road – either side of the road, a low stone wall. Today Daughty Moore sat there. She wore a summer dress, more suitable to one half her age. She had a light white cardigan and her legs crossed. Daughty was tanned from that year's summer and her hair in a tiny bun. Granny didn't like Daughty Moore or where she sat.

"You have lovely grandchildren", Daughty politely remarked. *"You should be proud of them"*. Daughty was never married, never had children – seemed to remain a slip of a lassie all her life. That's hard to take, when you've had to pay the toll for seven kids and seven packets of ginger nuts a week. But what Daughty said was nice and nicely said. My granny sat with her and for the first time ever, they had a conversation – about the ages of the grandchildren. Granny told her about her other grandchildren in America and three in Manorhamilton; Peggy's three – said there was a little house for sale there – on Boley Hill – but it was very small. Daughty said small was good and easy kept. She invited Granny up to her house for a cup of tea and a biscuit. Granny said she would and she did.

Granny got a gunk when she saw the inside of Daughty's tiny cottage. Some part of her had wanted it to be distasteful – a Madam's Den – a place to bring The Egg Man – a place of sleaze and filth and fornication. It was anything but. It was bright and delicate – a room little girls dream of when they're playing 'Tea'. This was the only room apart from the bedroom and it was delightful. Granny and Daughty sipped from china cups – Granny ignored the offering of 'Marietta' biscuits – their value diminished by the pleasant company and easy conversation. Granny was beginning to see light.

CHAPTER 9

Operation Moving Granny

Margaret sat at the table in a clean tartan dress and white socks. We all knew they wouldn't stay up on her and that they wouldn't stay white for long. She had her hair combed and it made us all sad, seeing her look like this. She was starting school and she looked different and subdued and frightened and Margaret was never frightened.

She couldn't go to school. She was our ringleader, our instigator; how would we get into trouble without her. Her socks and shiny black shoes just looked silly and the white cardigan like Daughty Moore's. Who did she think she was? And she got an egg in a cup for her breakfast and bread and jam for her lunch. It was like she was being executed. Daddy had made up a special wooden shelf for the mudguard of the tractor, so that he could carry her to school on his way to the creamery.

Mammy told her to stand in the door in her outfit and new schoolbag. We never had a camera in our house, but Mammy always took a mental picture of us when we were taking a step out into the world.

It was a big blow for me to be losing my sister, so early in life. She sat on the wooden shelf thing and had her knees either side of the creamery can, a full load for the 'Twenty'. She didn't even wave goodbye; just put her arms around Daddy's neck and off they went. I stayed most of that day with Granny. She was busy writing letters - never went near a ginger nut the whole day. The next thing Mammy put me in the pram and me and her and Kevin walked over to Drumeela to meet Margaret coming out from school.

Margaret looked like she had been pulled through a hedge when she came running out, because she had been pulled through a hedge - several times. She was in the worst of bad humour. She said they called her horsey and that they ate her lunch and spat it back out because they said it was horrible. Mammy's bread and jam were not horrible, but then we didn't know what horrible was.

When we got back as far as the vegetable garden at the bottom of our lane, Mammy went in the near way and pulled three stalks of rhubarb and when we took up our positions at the kitchen table, she let us stick them in the sugar bowl and we ate them. I was six months at the time and had never had anything like it. I ripped the nappy out of it that night with sheer joy and rhubarb farts. We didn't think Margaret would go to school the next day, but she did - didn't put in as much time combing the hair, but she still went and continued to go and we were lost without her.

Margaret had just turned five and Kevin gone three, the years were flying by and I wasn't even one yet. Both their birthdays were lavish affairs – we had custard and jelly after dinner and Mammy made a sponge cake; we ate half of it at the end of July, for Margaret's birthday and the other half in September for Kevin's. It didn't seem as tasty the second time round. Mammy said that was because we were getting spoilt. We didn't walk to Drumeela to collect Margaret after that first day. She walked home – most of the way with Mary Lee and then she'd call in to see Daughty Moore – got biscuits and ate them herself. Our wild adventures were now crammed into the evenings and the weekends. Then it was time for digging the potatoes.

The potatoes were set in spring. Ridges and ridges and ridges of them, they were shoveled and shoveled again – then they were sprayed and sprayed again and then they were dug out of the ridge for the dinner; these were the new potatoes, *"Balls of flour"*, the Auld Lad would proclaim as he peeled the first. Then in September or October, it would be time to dig them all up and put them in a 'Heap' for the winter. My father would go along carefully with the spade and break away the soil and leave a trail of freshly dug spuds in his wake. It was our job – anyone who could walk that is – to pick the spuds into a bucket and carry them to the dry bank where the 'Heap' would be positioned. Enough potatoes to do us almost a year. And so, for what seemed like weeks and weeks, we were in the Pretta Field – digging.

Farming was great for breaking up the year. In the spring, we put out the dung - we planted the spuds and the garden. The cows calved and sucked and the milking started. In the summer, we mowed and made hay and saved the turf and went to football matches – In the autumn we brought in the hay, dug the spuds and thanked God for what we had. And in winter, we ate the spuds and held tight, we foddered and played cards. We looked forward to Christmas and beyond that, the Spring again – and we found the rhythm, a different rhythm to our daily one, but a rhythm all the same.

In spite of our best hopes, Margaret liked school. She went every day and she was happy there. She was eager to learn and take chances and explore and although we missed her from our weekday lives, we took stock of her development and tried to follow as best we could.

As that winter approached, we knew something was afoot. The rhythm of the house shifted – we weren't old enough to understand, but we knew there was something. Whispered conversation coming from the Auld Pair's room – Granny full time writing letters – Granny going to town – Granny visiting her daughter in Manorhamilton – Granny being nice – Granny laughing – Granny crying – Granny letting go.

My first Christmas came and went without a nudge. Margaret got a sewing set; Kevin got a ball – there was a smell of bacon and black pudding that hadn't been there before. Mammy and Granny ended the cold war

– a truce was found. They found that their paths were not encroaching on one another, but running parallel and in the same direction. And then we turned into 1966. I was about to turn the grand old age of one. But first, that January, there was a momentous day. Granny was going – leaving – moving out. She had bought that little house on Boley Hill in Manorhamilton. She would spend the next twenty years there. Our house was upset.

A hitch had been fitted to the car. A trailer was borrowed from Big Ned and then it was time for Operation Moving Granny. A wooden chest full of moth balls was first. Armfuls of clothes; coats; a clatter of hats; undergarments that marched out themselves; shoes and dresses that hinted at a younger woman with spark and promise. Then all that was left was the fragile stuff – the china – the tea-sets – the vases – the jewelry – the teeth. When sorting and fussing stopped and the trailer was full, my grandmother was ready for off. She was ahead of schedule as she liked to be. Then she decided it was time for a cup of tea.

That was a strange moment for everyone, but for Mammy mostly. In the blink of an eye, my Granny went from being a member of our household – a member of my family, with her own things, her own place and her own way – to being a visitor. It was like someone waved a wand. All of a sudden, she sat in a different chair – my mother brought china from the parlour and with renewed vigour and kindness – made Granny tea. Granny excelled in her new role as guest and made jokes and laughed and she and my mother, for once, threw their energies into a positive embrace. I almost cried out *"That's more like it, girls"*, but I was only ten months at the time and it would have sounded a bit cheeky.

Granny's belongings did not fit into Big Ned's two-cow trailer – there'd have to be another run done – or maybe two. She gave us each a half a crown – only Mammy took mine in case I'd swallow it. Then my granny up'd and left. The Auld Lad transported her to her new home in two full loads. That was the day Granny started to enjoy life. First, she let go and then she learned to fly – like a blackbird from a field of corn and she was majestic.

I was devastated – who was going to mind me? First, I lost my sister to the idea of learning and personal improvement and now my poor grandmother was gone. I was left in a cloud of dust and emotion. I had nowhere to turn. Mammy was too busy. Daddy had to shave and Kevin was only three. The only thing left, was to grow up – and fairly rapidly. I needed to practice my walking.

In rural Ireland, we all walk a bit funny. The reason is, we usually learn at home on the farm or in the kitchen with farm animals. When I went in search of my walking technique, I had two choices; to walk like a pig or to walk like a chicken! I fell somewhere between the two. I was fat and roundy and the pig style suited me best, but when I went from four legs to two – I kept falling over. That's when I started to study the chicken. I know I've mocked my father's dancing; well it was nothing to my early walking. For years I walked like I had just laid an egg in my trousers!

Learning to do physical stuff keeps your mind occupied. When you're a child, it's all go and a good job too. If you had time to lie back in your nappy and take it all in, you'd go mad. I was a good baby, robust and quiet – never said a word till I was nearly two. I wasn't good on my feet and so I couldn't stand in gaps yet, but you could park my pram there and that worked just the same.

And what's the big deal with standing in gaps? Well, every field has a gap to the road or the lane or into the next field. When you move the cattle or cows from one part of the farm to another – someone needs to stand in the gaps. It's one of the main reasons you have children in the first place.

CHAPTER 10

Minding Eggs

On the ninth of May 1968, my youngest sister was born. She would be the last. We had enough now. Two boys, two girls and a 'Twenty Tractor' – what more help could you need? My new sister was named Geraldine and she was great. I was now three. Kevin had started school and I was on my own during the day and it was pure torture. Not a thing to be at, apart from play blind mans buff with the dish-cloth. We had two bricks of Lego that Margaret found on the road and a marble that she stole. The Lego bricks didn't fit into each other, but you could put them into your mouth, one at a time or the two together. I could have put a lot more into my mouth, if we'd had them, but Margaret or Kevin couldn't find any more. Kevin had a hump on him from looking for Lego. The marble was out of commission, Mammy took it off me after I pegged it at McCaffery one night, when he was cheating at cards.

Daddy was fierce fond of Geraldine, because she was the first out and out girl. Margaret was a girl too, but because of me and Kevin and having to do so much farm work, she had turned into a bit of a tom-boy and wasn't near as cute as her younger sister. Still Margaret was the leader and if ever anything went wrong, we'd all put on our innocent heads and look at her and she'd get the blame. There was three years of a gap between me and Geraldine and the pram was in an awful state. We were now using it for general farm work. Bringing locks of hay to cows and delivering cement blocks to Daddy when he was building the wall at the pigsty; collecting eggs, drawing water and free-wheeling down to Clogher Cross, just for the jig of it. When Mammy was about to pop with Geraldine, not only did the car have to be serviced, but we had to jack up the pram and give it the mother and father of all cleanings. We had to fill the tank several times afterwards.

Geraldine was put in the Girls' Room from the start. That was the top half of the house full now. Two girls in the Girls' Room – two boys in the Boys' Room – Mammy and Daddy in the room beside the landing – and the biggest landing in South Leitrim and room to no one. Of course, downstairs, we still had the spare room – Granny's old room – the Good Room – the room in case of visitors – or – the room if someone got sick. We weren't allowed into that room, but I used to look in every now and again, just to remind myself of what a tidy room looked like.

I went in one morning and there was John Maguire sitting up in the bed drinking a mug of tea. I got an awful shock. No one was allowed to drink mugs of tea in bed and why would you want to? I said, *"Hello Grandad"*, and closed the door. I was waiting for an explanation, but there wasn't one. Our house wasn't one of those houses where there were big discussions around the table or family meetings. So, none of us knew what was going on. To this day, I don't know where Grandad came out of. But that was it, he was now living in our house – in the spare room mostly – and sometimes sitting in Granny's chair, taking tea and eating out of our pot. He was good company. He didn't eat as much as Granny and he didn't mind us like Granny did, but we laughed more and lit his 'Woodbines'.

Of course, we were too young to notice, but Grandad wasn't in great form at the time – whatever that meant. Youngsters don't digest vague remarks like that. We just wanted something or someone to push in the pram and now we had Geraldine and I knew loads of tricks I could do with her, but some of them would have to wait till her hair grew a bit longer.

I don't know whether it was having all the help or because of an upturn in the country's economy, but Daddy started to think about making improvements on the farm. There was talk of a new cattle mart being built in Carrigallen – it would be the first of it's kind in the region. Margaret and Kevin were bringing home stories from school of televisions and being able to watch a man reading the news and football matches and

Muhammad Ali – whoever he was. For the first time in our lives, the outside world was nibbling inwards and for so long it had been just us nibbling out. It was exciting and confusing. Why did we need change?

The Sixties were nearly over and Leitrim or at least our part of Leitrim hadn't been budged by Flower Power, or Free Love or Vietnam or Bob Dylan or the Beatles or the Rolling Stones. Only John F Kennedy had knocked at our window and Pope Paul the sixth. Two powerful men, but two good ones or so we were told. Our development was going to take shape in the form of a new byre. It would be built alongside the hayshed and there would be place for sixteen cows. Pure madness – how could anyone expect to gather up sixteen cows and how would we milk them? By hand for now – the Auld Lassie had eight year's training – but the Auld Lad was thinking ahead. He was planning on getting a milking machine – but then what would Mammy do?

A foundation was dug out for a new byre and a dairy – and that was it for now. Everything around our house was built in stages. First, we thought about it – that could take up to four years. Then we dug the foundation. Then we let it settle – that could go on for another year or two. Then we'd make a decision whether to go ahead or not. Sometimes we did, sometimes we didn't. Few people at the time, but some, took out loans and sometimes they bridged that loan with another loan. We didn't even borrow a crow-bar and we bridged everything with time.

I was minding my sister by the range. She was only a week home from the hospital, I could hear Grandad coughing in the room. Mammy was outside finishing up, doing the things. Kevin was chasing hens. Daddy was at the creamery and Margaret was letting out the cows. It was a Saturday in May. The early spring had been fierce cold and wintery. The weather was only gettin' goin'. The Auld Pair had a slither of jobs lined up, now that all the help was home.

"Any sign of your sister?" That's the first I heard of it. I said, *"Still asleep"*, but that wasn't the sister my mother meant. It was confusing having two. Then Mammy came in again and put on eggs and told me to mind them. I hated minding eggs, because there's very little difference between the look of a hard-boiled egg and a soft one. Kevin came in exhausted from the hens. He was only sitting when Mammy came back and told him to go to the well – that Margaret was lost and we needed water for the tea. *"The next thing your father will be home from the creamery"* – Mammy was great at predicting things. She was right, the next thing, we could hear the tractor coming over the road. That'd be Daddy. Mammy came back then and told me to see if Grandad wanted anything. And how was them eggs coming along and did the baby wake yet and I could be buttering bread, if I had nothing else to do.

I took off the eggs – no one was going to eat an egg if it was too hard and if it was too soft – I was only three – what did they expect? Grandad was looking for a mug of tea, he was fierce fond of tea. I told him there'd be no tea till Kevin came back from the well. He wasn't happy, but I couldn't make water. Then Mammy and Daddy came in and sat down and looked at each other. That was strange. Kevin came back from the well and there was tea made. No sign of Margaret. Mammy brought Grandad tea – he'd have a Woodbine in the room. I had bread buttered and we all had our breakfast in silence. Geraldine was a great child and didn't wake up and wasn't lost like her sister. Mammy said I made a good job of the eggs – there was one left. An egg going to loss, because our Margaret couldn't be found.

The Auld Pair looked at each other again – that was twice in the one day – something was up. Margaret O'Rourke was missing since she went off with the cows. Children only get called by their full names when they're in trouble. Margaret was always called Margaret O'Rourke. It was an hour since she had gone missing – just enough time for us to have the breakfast and decide what to do next. First, they decided to go looking for her. Then, to wait for her to come back – that she always came back – but she had never been lost before. Then we all went outside and started shouting her name and searching – in the shed; the byre; the hayshed; down by the pool beside the bit of an orchard where the plum trees were and the Bamboo bush. Grandad stood at the back door and asked every time any of us went by, *"Any sign, no?"* Daddy went out the fields towards where the cows were. The baby cried – Mammy had to go into the house. Grandad finished another fag and went in after her. Me and Kevin went to look for Daddy.

It was the first tragedy to strike our family. Me and the brother were sad enough about the loss of our sister and wondered who'd get the egg. Then we heard a rattling of a plough and a horse. It was coming from Donald Murray's field. Donald was ploughing for oats. He had his big mare harnessed to the plough. It was such a sight. We had seen it before – last year. This field was on the brow of a hill. Donald was six foot seven and his mare was seventeen hands high – when they ploughed along the headland it was like they were ploughing on top of the world. We moved to get a better look. That's when we noticed Margaret sitting on the ditch watching what we were watching. Daddy came whistling – not because he was happy, but because that's what he did when he didn't know what to do. Margaret said, *"Come and look at Don's mare"*. And we did. There was no hugging or anything like that, because it turned out that Margaret wasn't lost at all – just watching Don's mare, and us after rushing the breakfast.

CHAPTER 11

The Short Chapter

The Auld Fella dropped us off at Drumeela National School. There was no creamery that day, so he brought the four of us over in the car. Geraldine came too, sitting on Daddy's lap the whole way – she was the lucky one. She was only one. It was September 1969, my first day at school, I was four – a big four, Kevin was seven and Margaret eight. I couldn't get over how tall everything was – the doors were tall, the ceilings were tall, the windows were tall – my hopes were tall. There'd be some craic today. I had a schoolbag with nothing but my lunch – wheaten bread and jam. Come on Drumeela – I'm ready if you are!

There were sixty or so childer going to Drumeela school. That number would increase rapidly over the next few years. Anyone who wasn't a bachelor or a spinster at the time, were making babies goodo. The headmaster was Tommy Moran and he knew lots of Irish and spellings and sums, but he couldn't work out where all the childer were coming from – a lot of use he was. We were told Master Moran could be a handful and he was... just about. He came in for a gander at the new arrivals. Most of us had older siblings at the school, so we could see the disappointment in his eyes as he made the connections. He said I looked like a very thick child and he was right, because although I was excited to be starting school – I had decided to go with the stubborn look that morning, just so I wouldn't get anyone's hopes up – and I didn't. The Master went off to try and straighten out the ones in the Big Room and we were left in the Small Room. The teacher in the Small Room was a sub – she was a wicked auld yoke that had come out of retirement to mind us, while the nice teacher was on maternity leave. That was the trouble with nice teachers, they were always having babies or at home watering flowers. This one wouldn't know what to do with a flower, if she had one.

There were fourteen others starting that day. That was a pity – I liked the bit of attention, but that wasn't going to happen. We had to sit at a desk – in the same place – for the whole day. I wasn't expecting that and we were told to ask when we wanted to go to the toilet. That was a problem for me, because sometimes I didn't know when I wanted to go, until I had already gone. The mistress wanted us to put up our hand and go through some formal ritual before being excused. I piddled on myself, twice in the first half hour. She was strangely amused, as were the class, when she announced –

sniggering – that I had had a little accident. I was fuming!

I decided they could stick their school – that's how thick I was. There was no need for making a laugh of childer like that. My class was full of other big lads – just as thick as me. Hugh Joseph Morgan Reilly had enough names for half a class. John Prior; he was a real buck – the Priors wouldn't know which end of them was up. The Lees – Michéal and James could melt into any surroundings. The Shannons – Gerard and John were twins, but looked more like their sisters than they did each other. John McGerty was fulltime going about thinking – that wasn't very acceptable at our school. Some never thought – just talked non-stop – you were as well off saying nothing. They were going to treat us like childer, whether or no. Most of us could already drive a tractor and wheel turf and mind the house. The piddling in our trousers was only because of nervousness in front of strangers. It turned out I was the only one was nervous. There were a few girls in our new class too – but we kept away from them. I knew from home, that girls were trickier and they were the ones that laughed the most when I wet myself! Then it was breaktime.

I was looking forward to breaktime, but it turned out breaktime was only Little Break and not for eating your lunch. I had most of mine gone already and wanted to finish it off, but the Master caught me looking into the schoolbag. I decided not to eat the lunch – out of spite and I never looked into the schoolbag more. He told me to play with the other childer, but what was there to play? There was only auld tig and running around in circles, like what they'd be at out in Africa. There was a bit of concrete at the back of the school and a shed – that was our playground. The outside toilet was there too and a bit of hilly ground where we played football. The ball was always going over the wall into the open tank of the toilet or out onto the road. You were as well idle as playing football at yon school.

There was a big bee in the window of the infant's room that first day – trying to get out. All the kids were sitting colouring and writing and putting up their hands and the bee stuck in the corner of the window, buzzing. I tried to let him out, but I was told to sit back in my seat – as if the school was going to take off and everyone needed to be in their place. John Prior had as little interest in what was going on as me – he tried to sell me a cow that we could see over on Annagh hill. It belonged to John Lynch and John Prior wanted a penny for her. I didn't have a penny that day. Where would I get a penny? He told me to try me father's pockets. I wondered how I'd get the cow home and where I'd put her and what would Mammy and Daddy say? Then we had to do colouring – I was no good at colouring.

We walked home after school – that was the best part. A clatter of us headed back the Drumbrick Road. The Lynches, the Dolans, the Lees, the O'Kelly's, Tomás Mimna, my brother and sister and me. Most of them branched off along the way until it was just us and

Tomás. Tomás was our friend and second cousin from up the road towards Drumreilly.

This journey should have taken half an hour, if our minds were on walking and the many crucial jobs that lay in wait at home – but it didn't – it took a good two hours most evenings – sometimes less and the odd time – three hours. It was because of those same jobs that we dilly-dallied and picked blackberries and robbed Patterson's orchard and locked Edmond Patterson in his shed and jumped on the back of Alan Taylor's low trailer that he used for the creamery run. Sometimes we went to Daughty Moore's for a drink of water, when all we really wanted was a few 'Marietta' biscuits – sometimes we found her and the 'Egg Man' hard at it down by Clogher river. That's what *he* had to do for a biscuit. Mostly, we just kicked up our heels and enjoyed that wonderful time between Drumeela and home. Anything was better than school or work on the farm.

I have always imagined that school and the activities surrounding it would form a big part of any recounting of my life, but it doesn't. When I go searching – I only find embers of negativity and spite, embarrassment and shame and uncontrolled piddling. That's no one's fault. I couldn't be taught. I put up a guard the first day I went there and I didn't take it down till the day I left. I learned to read and write – just about. I learned how to act the clown. I always had my lunch before first break. School is not for everyone – but everyone has to eat.

CHAPTER 12

McCaffery

On a cold, wet, drizzly day in 1970 – a Saturday – the 7th of February, I walked up the road past McCaffery's to Tomás Mimna's house. His father, Tom was a brother of Christy's and a first cousin of my father. Tomás was my boyhood friend and neighbour. He was fifteen months older than me, but was still the nearest playmate in age and distance. Anyway, I was big for my age, so that usually added a year in those days. It was my turn to go up to him. We lived roughly three hundred yards apart and we took turns in visiting each other. Today it was me. Tomás was an only child, so he'd have his jobs to do – no point in going there before 11am.

When he came to our house, we played made-up games – like jumping across the pool beside the orchard or sticking sticks in cow dung and chasing each other around the Haggard. When the weather was good, we'd go rambling up Baxter's Hill and through the old gardens and be kings. At his house it was more organised and straightforward. When the weather was fine Beesie, Tomás's mother would find us a nice handy job around the house – clipping hedges or pulling weeds – but we'd get soda bread and rhubarb jam – a lot more often than if I was at home. Beesie was a light slip of a woman, she was great fun and fond of tea, because she smoked. She didn't expect me to have the bread and jam every time there was tea, but I did, because I wouldn't get it at home. When the weather was bad like today – we'd go into their work shed and play. Their shed was tidier than our kitchen and Tomás had no end of proper toys. Toy trucks and cars and soldiers. Lego that came in a box and fitted together. Police cars with sirens and batteries. We weren't allowed to abuse these toys or take them apart or peg them against the wall, but still, it was great to see what proper toys looked like.

Before I'd go home, I'd be brought down to the room to show me the television. They had it this while and Beesie would get Tomás to tell me about some of the programmes that would be on later in the evening, as they didn't turn it on till after the milking. It was the first telly I'd ever seen, but would have to wait a while before I could see it working. Then it was time for me to go – Tomás would have more jobs to do and Beesie would be longing for another cup of tea and I had enough eaten. Time to go home. We said our goodbyes and I headed off.

McCaffery was sitting on the ditch along the road under his house. That time, it was a familiar sight to see some of these men sitting along the side of the road. It might seem incomprehensible now, but back then, logical enough. If you lived in a dark and dingy cottage with no light or radio and you weren't on speaking terms with your brother – your best chance of getting a bit of news or company, was along the road. They'd sit and hope that someone would be coming from town with news or lies or scandal. Today wasn't a pleasant day for sitting out, and today McCaffery didn't want news. He had another agenda. He was abrupt as always.

"Where are ya going, young fella?"

"Home"

"Will ya go to the shop for me?"

"Why – sure aren't you here!"

I knew what McCaffery was asking, it's just I had never been to the shop on my own, I wasn't even sure of the way. I was big for my age, but I still wasn't five yet. McCaffery knew he was pushing his luck, but he was desperate for fags.

"Go down and ask your mother, does she want anything from the shop? Come back up to me then."

I hurried home and found my mother knitting in the kitchen. She said I'd have to go if McCaffery asked me to go. She wasn't pleased with him – but there was no such thing as turning down a neighbour in distress. I wasn't happy either. I had longed to go to the shop, but I wanted to go on my terms and with someone to guide me – this was looking like a lone voyage. Where was my big sister or my brother – they were off gallivanting with Geraldine, because she was now the cute one and I was left to plough my own furrow. Being four and a good bit was not an easy age. I was handed the shopping bag and some coins and told to get corned beef and a packet of soup – Oxtail – very fancy. But where exactly was the shop?

Hyland's shop or Corrawallen Post Office, as it was officially known was three quarters of a mile up the road, no stops, no turn off's, *"Just keep going and you'll find it and don't be long"*.

I headed off – McCaffery was still on the ditch wondering where I was. He told me to get ten 'Sweet Afton' – a half quarter of tobacco and a bar of Dairy Milk chocolate. I was aware that this man was a knave and a rogue and a half quarter didn't sound like a valid quantity to me. I repeated, *"A half quarter"*. He could see the confusion in my eyes and asked was I deaf. He shoved paper money into my fist and said that Clare would know and hurry up. I was raging – that was no way to explain to a not very bright, fat four-year-old. He could have wrote it down or could he not go himself? He was well able to go to town or Gorby's for a feed of porter, but couldn't make his way to the shop. The only thing that saved him was the chocolate – that *had* to be for me.

I have walked, cycled and driven more times to Hyland's shop over the years and it has never been a chore – except for that day. That first day I was petrified – for loads of reasons – that I wouldn't find it – that there was no such thing as a half-quarter – that I wouldn't have enough money – that I'd wet myself. Too late. Never mind – it was still drizzling and I had other things to worry about. I passed the turn-down for Drumshangore Bog, by Toome Lane, Hugh Murray's was on the left and then Mrs. Woods' pretty cottage. Where was the shop? I had nearly piddled on myself a second time before I got to the end of the road. Now where? The Clogher road joins the main Carrigallen-Ballinamore road at an angle. Back to my left was Carrigallen and to my right was sort of straight on, but meant joining another road. No one mentioned joining another road. *"Just go straight"*, my mother said! I took a chance and went to my right and there it was – Corrawallen Post Office.

This was a rural shop – an oasis – a tower of respectability that stood high above the drudgery and begrudgery of the time and place. The place we assembled for pension and provision – for encouragement and assistance – where we got our bits and left our troubles. Today would be my first time through the door. A bell sounded. There was no one there. A counter left and right and straight ahead. A meat slicer and weighing scales, a freezer and a fridge. There were nice things and practical things hanging side by side, like there was no differ between the two, but I knew otherwise. Why could we not get nice things too? I steadied myself. This was not my current conundrum – my mission today was, first – to find the way – done – now to get McCaffery's things bought, paid for and delivered with as little fuss as possible. Clare came through to the shop from the kitchen. She had her apron on – she would never be without it.

"Ah you must be young Rourke; I'd know you out of your father".

I was relieved that I was known and welcomed. I asked for ten Sweet Afton.

"You must be shopping for McCaffery?"

More good news.

"You probably want a half quart of Golden Virginia too?"

"I do", says I. *"And a bar of Dairy Milk Chocolate, please"*. I paid for McCaffery's things with McCaffery's money and then I got the soup and corned beef. I was fascinated with the slicer. I paid in more coins and got coins back. I wasn't sure which money was in which pocket – but Clare gave me a lollypop on account of it being my maiden voyage and I was away off down the road with a smirk on my face. Maybe I wasn't so reliant on my big sister and brother after all. They could have Geraldine, now that I was a big boy, able to go to the shop on my own. I was happy out.

McCaffery was still sitting on the ditch. I thought he must have a wet bottom. I gave him his cigarettes; tobacco; his one bar of lovely chocolate and a good go of change. He scolded. Had I no idea of what change to give him? Then he started going through the 'times tables' with me. I was lost – we had only done counting at school. He said I couldn't go home till it was sorted out. He was back to his knave'n, but sure I didn't know that. I started crying and piddling at the same time. He just thought it was tears running down my leg. I had my short trousers on and it was hard to hide my shame. He said I shouldn't be going to the shop, if I couldn't do me tables. He sorted out the money and told me I had him robbed. He gave me the chocolate and said I wasn't to have any, that it was for my mother when she was having her tea. I wasn't overly fond of McCaffery after that. I knew Mammy wouldn't eat the chocolate, but I knew if I gave it to her, she'd only divide it up. I had gone through too much for that to happen. When I got a little way down the road. I sat on the ditch like McCaffery. And I ate the chocolate and finished it off with two slices of corned beef. Mammy never knew a thing.

CHAPTER 13

Our Field of Dreams

Where we lived was a hundred yards off the road. A white wooden fence ran from the road along the lane and arched around at the front of the dwelling. Inside the railing was a small sweet meadow that sat directly in front of the house. In the middle of this was a tall and mighty ash tree. We called it 'The Field in Front of the House'. It was never mowed. We let the calves in there in the spring; handy for keeping an eye on them. When the calves were gone, it became our sports field. Mostly football, but also show-jumping with pretend horses, tennis with pretend rackets (or sticks), and the Leitrim dominated autumn sport of catching leaves.

For the Christmas of 1970, me and the brother got a leather football between us. A ball in December around our place was like getting a cigarette and no matches. We had no place to play. Everywhere was too wet. It was the old style leather ball with a lace and a bladder. It was not fully round and doubled in weight when wet.

Kevin was mad for football – I wasn't that pushed. Every now and then, we'd take it out and pass it to one another without letting it bounce. If a leather ball was bounced on a stone street, that was the end of it, or so we were told. We forgot about it for a while, or at least I did, and then winter turned to spring and on a day in May when the calves were gone from the field there was a row down by the Haggard between me and my brother. I don't recall what it was about – probably some meaningless job that I didn't want to help with and the two of us squared up to each other. He was older, but I was almost as big. He knocked lumps off me. I lay in a heap in the nettles - Kevin felt sorry for me then and called a truce. That's when he suggested we bring the leather ball to the field in front of the house.

I was gone six, he was a good eight. The day was middling and the field was soft. We both had wellingtons on and still in short trousers. We climbed the fence and stood twenty yards apart. We started kicking the ball over and back to each other. We did this for a while – we thought it was a while, but it was in fact – hours. Maybe it was because of the row – maybe it was our need to make up. Two brothers connected through our kicking and catching of an off-round football. A link, maybe our only link, it's certainly been our strongest link to this day.

And we treated this piece of leather like glass – we knew there would be no replacement if anything happened it. From the word go, we made our kicks accurate and our hands safe. No extra wear and tear, meant more hours in the field in front of the house, playing football. I was now hooked on this damn sport that would fill me up and rip me apart. There were times when I wished my brother had left me in the nettles.

Our mother called us for our tea – no remarks passed on the hours we had spent – not doing something useful. At tea, Daddy asked was the ball any good. We said it was. We didn't mention that it swerved about mid-flight. And then he said, *"Yez may get football boots"* – as if we had our own money and could go to Ballinamore in the morning. Mammy asked what colour did Leitrim wear. I didn't know and neither did my brother. That took a tut from the Auld Lad. *"Green and Gold like Kerry – but without the medals".*

The next morning when we got up for school, there were two pairs of green and yellow football socks on the table. Mammy had knitted them. We put them on and we couldn't take them off, they were so woollen and so soft inside in our wellingtons as we headed off to school. The wellingtons I had before these had a hole in the sole and my sock used to flap out, but not these – these were Kevin's old wellies and the sock stayed in and at break time when we played football, I kicked straighter than I had ever kicked before. It was the wool.

Then 'Home Time' came – and for the first time in my two years at school, I didn't want to go home – I wanted to play football. We had a plastic ball at school that could be kicked anywhere and against anything. The others were not so keen and were already gone up the road. When I came out, they were at O'Brien's shed, beckoning me to hurry up. Sitting on the ditch between the school and O'Brien's was John McCarron and his post war stress thing that he did.

John was the man who disrupted Mass and walked about pulling things out of hedges and talked to himself and had the head movements of a chicken. He didn't seem to communicate in the normal way. He didn't really communicate at all. The older men used to say – if you got him on his own, he'd talk normal enough. This was my chance. I was on a high from the woollen socks and the straight kicking and I had an audience. I called to my school companions and said I'd be with them in a minute, that I just wanted to have a chat with my friend here. They were impressed at my bravery. John McCarron was said to have hand grenades in his pockets. My sister Margaret was not so impressed – I valued her opinion, but I had already committed to this dare – and what could he do – he was a regular Mass goer – he wasn't going to shoot me – I hoped.

Because of our youth and our pre-formed ideas of villains and weirdos – we never really looked properly at these people, or at least I didn't. It so happens John McCarron was a tall rangy man – square shouldered and athletic. A bit of a film star look about him – apart from his tics and his gauldering. He never bothered anyone and never hung around the school. Today, it seems, he just got his timing wrong. He was sat on the ditch with his back to Annagh Hill. I stopped when I got as far as him – my siblings and companions looked on with bated breath. I had to say something.

"*Well John*", I said all brash. I stood in the middle of the road and stared at this poor helpless man. He looked up and our eyes met. You never know till you look into the eyes of someone, what you're going to find. It brought me back a peg or two. I thought I was being all brave – grasping the nettle – taking the bull by the horns. I wasn't. I was just a fat, annoying child in short trousers and woollen football socks – a brat, and that's what I saw in his eyes. Not some mysterious sadness or loneliness or hopelessness. I looked into this man's eyes and they were saying. *"Would you ever get away from about me, you annoying little child"*.

Our world growing up was full of weird and wonderful people. Oddities – too much brains – not enough brains – a bit slow – he got a bad fall – his mother left him in the room too long – bad with her nerves – a home boy – just not right – some little thing. They were everywhere. I have unreliably been told that Leitrim had the most people per capita in mental institutions at that time. I'm not talking about those; I'm talking about the ones who couldn't get in. John McCarron was one of them, but John McCarron had put me in my place with a look and I took him up on it and went home as quick as I could.

When we got home, the Auld Fella had left three long straight-ish ash poles by the fence at the front of the house. These poles would make a great set of goalposts. On Saturday, we were brought to Frank

O'Brien's in Ballinamore and got a pair of 'Blackthorn' football boots each. On Sunday we went to see Crosserlough playing in Breffni Park in Cavan. Our GAA adventure had started.

On Sunday evening, when we got back from Breffni, the Auld Fella brought out the crowbar and a bit of twine and started work on the goalposts. It was one of the few times I was interested in work. I stood beside him as he stripped down to his vest and began to bury the crowbar in the soft ground. We erected the two uprights. I took one end of the crossbar; Kevin took the middle and the Auld Man hoisted the other end to roughly six foot and tied it with the twine. He took out his pen-knife – he always impressed me with that– and he snipped off the excess. He came to my side then, and lifted me and the crossbar up to match the other end. What a man – what strength – what height. We tied the second side and at last we had goalposts. Kevin was fierce excited and started doing chin-ups on the crossbar. The Auld Lad dared me do ten – I couldn't even do one. I had to let go. He told me I was like an old woman and that I'd never be any good if I couldn't do a chin-up. I ignored his remark and put on my football boots and socks. We had one set of goalposts; a leather ball and we had the memory of the game in Breffni Park embedded in our brains.

We also had the names of the players. Kevin was Andy McCabe and I was Gene Cusack and we played with the hunger and zeal of that famous Crosserlough team – seven-in-a-row – Champions! Earlier that day, we had admired the speed and skill of these men, but also, we couldn't help but be taken in with the atmosphere in the ground. The roar of the crowd, my father's intensity when a move was coming together. *"Whisht... whisht... whisht..."*, he leaned forward in anticipation. The game excited him as it did me and my brother. The arena – the noise – the winning and losing – but more than all that – this game affected people. It affected my father.

And now, on a bright summer's evening under his watchful eye – the field in front of the house became our Field of Dreams. We ran and side-stepped, jumped, blocked and intercepted and the crowd roared. Boy did they roar, because the crowds at our imaginary games were never anything other than bewildered at our skill and bravery and style. I commentated, *"The ball comes to Cusack, he turns, he goes by one, two, three men and fires it over the bar"*. Daddy asked, *"Who are you?"*, I said *"Gene Cusack"*, he said, *"Mmm – I think you're more like John McCarron"*.

CHAPTER 14

Kate Dolan

After Mass every Sunday, the Auld Fella would get the Sunday paper in Kate Dolan's. Kate's was the shop and Post Office beside Drumeela Chapel. Kate had come from Glangevlin in County Cavan. A part of the country well renowned for tough Christians and Kate was tough and rough. She was single and never been kissed, not even by her mother. She looked like she had gone to seed. Her tiny shop had lots that few wanted. It was the clattiest dive you'd dare go into. The postman was Benny Brady, a great darts player, he must have learned his precision from picking his steps through Kate's shop. People bought the paper there and childer bought sweets. The bread man would come every day and leave in a few batch loaves. These loaves were still warm from the oven. Kate's cat, 'Rascal' loved them. The cat sat on the bread to keep herself warm and then she kept the bread warm till someone bought it. There was a fridge for ice-cream and Mr Freezes – the liquid variety. She had penny-bars and 'Blackjacks', 'Pink-Panthers' and stuck-together sweets. She still had 1½p Taytos when they were 3p anywhere else. She had rat poison for sale and rat poison to eat in. Rascal was not a rat cat. Kate also had some land and a few cows that she milked by hand and a byre that she was accused of cleaning out by hand – with her bare hands. She never washed her hands. She had no matching footwear – a sandal and a slipper – a wellington and a shoe. Her hair was made from steel-wool. That was Kate. A description of Kate sounds exaggerated in recall, but at the time, there were lots like her. Without outside influence – some women let themselves go – some women didn't go to the hairdressers or the barbers or the sink. Hair like a whin bush, was how the master described May Quinn, Mary Stormey and one Kate Dolan.

The master was the headmaster at our school – Tommy Moran. He was a great GAA man. Indeed, a man of many talents. He was an inter-county referee, a revered amateur actor with the Carrigallen Community Players, a great wit and someone who gave generously of his time to every organization the length and breadth of Leitrim and beyond. He had a car and a leather coat. When he had the leather coat on, you could look out. Whatever it was about that coat, it made him change – become impatient with the likes of me and Micky Lee and John Prior. And who could blame him? He was a man destined for better things – instead he had to listen to us yahooing and side-stepping our way through the education system. How do you deal with a crowd who refused to apply themselves to English, Irish, reading or spelling? We had no interest in History, Geography, sum, or catechism and we hated Irish dancing.

Mrs Coffey used to come one day a week with a bun on her head and kisses for all the boys. She had a yellow Volkswagen Beetle and taught Irish dancing. 'The walls of Limerick', 'The Siege of Ennis' and the 'Back one, two, threes'. It cost 5p, that we didn't have and Master Moran NT paid for most.

The only thing we could do or showed any interest in was football. He fired half a dozen of us into the car one evening after school and brought us to Carrigallen. It was our first official football match. At the age of seven, I had scored a goal for the under 12's – Kevin was nine and played in defence. Brian Brady was somewhere between me and Kevin and scored fourteen goals a game! He was the postman's son and the best footballer at our school by a mile. That was it, organized football had started. We practiced all the time – sometimes in Drumeela – sometimes in Carrigallen. We were never late – we were never busy at home. Geraldine was now four and in her second year at school. She had started when she was three, because she couldn't be kept away. She was big enough to go and she went. She was big enough to go to the well and help with hay and stand in gaps, so why not go to school

One evening after football, I found myself at Drumeela on my own. Kevin had ran off home to help do the things. The Lees were gone too. All gone. That often happened – I'd have drifted into some sort of a stupor and lost track of time – awake but not fully with it – gone to some place in my mind where there was absolute stillness and calmness and quiet – and then I'd come-to and my lift would be gone. I'd like to say that this was a deep and meaningful experience, but it wasn't. It just meant that I had been walking around in a daze – *"With a big mopey head on ya"*, my mother would say.

This evening I was thirsty, I'd love a Coke, I thought. I didn't know what Coke tasted like, but I had seen other ones drinking it and I could see the smug sense of satisfaction on their faces. I wanted one – but I had no money. John Prior had told me that you could touch up Kate Dolan for stuff and tell her you'd pay her tomorrow. Now was the time to put that to the test. It was late and she mightn't be open, but it was worth a try. I went over and the door was off the latch. I went in – no sign of anyone – even the cat was gone to bed. There was a strip of fly catcher taking it's last breath. There was a hum off everything except the fridge. Suddenly Kate appeared in her negligée. Sexy as a cat sitting on a warm batch loaf.

"Fhat' do ya want?"

"Can I have a can a Coke and I'll pay you tomorrow"

"You can have a drink of Coke from that can there, someone left it behind them"

"Can I have a full one please and I'll pay you tomorrow"

"When is tomorrow?"

"Sorry... "

"They're all goin' to pay me tomorrow, I'd hate to miss it"

Kate put a can of Coke on the counter and asked who I was? When I told her that I was Jim Rourke's son, she replied with the usual reply when I told people who I was and where I was from. *"There's great big men about Drumeela".* There were great big men about Drumeela and I was proud that my Auld Fella was one of them.

Kate was like a celebrity. People laughed when you mentioned her – we all claimed to know her – but no one knew her. No one bothered to find out anything about her. Did she have family – was she ever a slip of a girl running about Glan and if so – how did she get from that to this. She was now in her sixties and lived like a pauper – when she died some years later – it was discovered, she had lots of money and left her shop to the parish. Kate's old shop was then done up and turned into a museum and a community centre. A place to have a cup of tea after a funeral or a special occasion. A nice way to remember this mad wonderful woman. You wouldn't drink a cup of tea in it when Kate had it – the cat would have the milk drank.

I didn't know how I was going to pay for this can of Coke. I had never got anything on spec before. I strolled over past the church with none of this on my conscience. It was getting dark. I stopped by the graveyard and went for it – my first can of Coke. I wiped the top of the filthy can with my snotty sleeve. I pulled the opener and Kate's Coke fizzed out the top –

lots of fizz – I was thirsty and I gulped it down. It made my head light. Warm and fizzy and sweet. My very own Coca Cola moment. A moment to savour on my own.

The graveyard wall was four-foot high at the road – only one-foot-high inside, in the graveyard behind me. It was on much higher ground. I stood with my back to the wall trying to make the bottom half of the Coke last longer than the top half. It was breezy and I could hear the conifers aching and swaying in the background. There was a pony neighing somewhere around Corglass – the same pony that neighed at funerals. I was almost finished my can. Almost time to crumple it up and peg it across the wall, like the big lads did. But something was keeping me there. Somehow, I wanted this moment to last. Was I beginning to like my own company? To experience the world at my own pace and on my own terms, without friends or family commentating on my progress. There's a peace in that and there was peace here. The gentle wind, the country sounds and then – the faintest sound of breathing or even sighing. I stood rigid against the wall. I could hear it plain. I was well used to ghost stories being bandied about around the fire at home. Was I about to be part of one? My very own ghost story. I was ready for it. *"Come on ghost, just don't drink my Coke"*. I stood in defiance. The breathing and the sighing got slightly louder and now there was an odour and I couldn't make it out. Was it souls waking from the dead? It smelt more like Kate Dolan. Then gently, a veil dropped down over my face. Was I about to be ascended into heaven? The only thing was, it still smelt like Kate Dolan – it was Kate Dolan! It was her negligée; she was sitting on the wall behind me – praying in the graveyard.

This was worse than any ghost. I was afraid to look up in case I'd have another 'Granny washing herself experience'. One thing for sure, I couldn't crumple up my Coke can the way I had intended. I gathered my thoughts – quickly and quietly and then with great certainty, I took a few very long and silent steps towards Drumbrick and when I knew I was out of danger, I ran like the bejapers.

At the Forge Bray, I was out of breath and free. No man or boy had ever had his head where I'd had mine. I couldn't tell anyone, because no one would believe me – but I was there and now I felt I knew Kate Dolan better than most. I know she was a Post Mistress and like all Post Mistresses of the time – she probably opened letters and listened in on phone calls and yes, she was a clatty auld yoke – the smell off her drawers was a terror – and undefinable. But I knew from first-hand experience – that, when work was done and when she was ready for bed – she sat on Drumeela graveyard wall and prayed for our dead.

CHAPTER 15

Purple

Geraldine needed help with her homework and I was the only one who knew the workings of a school. I was eight and she was five. I hadn't grown to like school, but I had made a shield of indifference to protect me from it and it fitted like a glove. Of course, Geraldine didn't need help, she was well able to rub on her own soap. Helping her just got me out of household chores. The house was quiet – Grandad had been sick and now he was sleeping – we were told to keep it down. It was half four – we were home early from school that day – because no one was interested in robbing or racing or acting the buck. Grandad was always in his chair when we'd get home – he'd always ask, *"Any slaps? Any tips? Any sign of Auld Patterson? Any sign of Daughty Moore?"* – To all these questions, I'd reply, *"No"*, regardless of what went on that day or who I'd seen. A positive response would only lead to more questions and I didn't like being asked things.

Grandad had a fierce reputation for being good craic, but the jiz was gone out of him this long time. He was a good man – tried to be as little nuisance as possible and he was. He let the house get on with it and he was there for recollection and reassurance. His brothers; Bob and Eddie would call every once in a while, with their young ones and the place got elevated into a buoyant spree. Bottles of stout and good ones; egg sandwiches and tea – they were exhausting highlights in a house where expression and merriment were almost frowned upon.

Geraldine was Grandad's pet. She was Daddy's pet. And she was my pet, because I wanted to be 'as near as made no difference' to any petting that was going on. I was raging that she had taken my crown of 'The Youngest One' and not only wore it with more finesse, but wore it for longer. I would make her life hell. I tangled her hair in the egg-beaters – I threw her wellies in the well. I poured tea on her copybooks and I tripped her and said she fell. And sometimes we were best friends and sat on the hay in the hayshed and minded the cat's kittens or – like this evening – helping with homework and then watching for the telly to come on.

We had a television now – on the press. It only had one station – we got it for the moon landing in '69 when Geraldine was only one. Mammy's cousin, in Dublin – Rosaleen and her husband Dick, brought it down as a second-hand – Bush – a black and white. It scrolled and rolled and fuzzed and broke our hearts. This evening it was fierce bad – couldn't get it steady. we were told to leave it and bring in the tub. It wasn't Saturday night. It was only Friday night, but Mammy said we had to have a bath, because Grandad was on the way out. We thought he was going to Gorby's – the local pub – which was a funny place to go with a bad flu – and was it not him she should be washing instead of us? He didn't go, or near go – only coughed and spluttered the whole night and the next day.

On Sunday morning we all went to Mass, except Grandad. When we got back Dr Farrelly was coming down the lane – he said, *"Woodbines, the flu and a bad heart"* – Grandad was seventy-one and dying. Later that day twenty-six people were shot in Derry by the British Army – it was January 30th 1972 - Bloody Sunday and there were people coming to our house that we didn't even know and now suddenly, my mother was centre of attention. She never sought attention – she was never easy when it swung her way. She had instinctively dodged it for twenty-nine years and many years after. But this Sunday evening she bowed to it, not for herself, but for her poor father who lay in the spare room with the weirdest colour of paint imaginable – a sort of purple. My Grandfather was dying and people I didn't even know were being exposed to my family's complete lack of taste in decor.

We got fierce well fed that day. There was several fries – Mammy kept trying to help with the cooking, but some woman shooed her away – she should have let her at it – something about the fries that wasn't right, and then a real heavy sadness fell on the house. Everyone talked like their talk was being recorded. I couldn't get over how quiet it was. We were brought into the purple spare room and told to kneel at the bed – I wanted to get a look at Grandad first. He had his eyes closed, but he didn't look like he was asleep. He looked disappointed and a little bit cross. Grandad never got vexed. He always acted like he was a visitor and was glad of a bed. Now he was dead. I wasn't quite sure what that meant, but it made everyone act strange. Then the praying started. Some baldly man started saying out prayers – he had a different way of saying them – he joined all the words together and made it into a snake – hailmaryfullofgracethelordiswiththeegiveusthisdayour dailybread... The snake was coming to get us. Kevin and Margaret looked so solemn – like they were playing a game, but they weren't. It was a small room and everyone was on top of each other. There was a dodgy smell of some of the women and I looked at Mammy. I couldn't read her eyes – I usually could, but this was a different look. I made my funny face that always made her smile, but it only made her frown. Someone's belly rumbled and that was it – I burst out laughing – it wasn't one thing – it was everything – man dead – purple paint – red eyes – warbling prayer – funny tummy – dodgy fry.

Mammy gave me the best clatter you ever saw. She connected so clean and with such precision, that I never felt a thing, yet it sent me flying across the room into someone's coat. Everyone was looking at me as if I was the boldest boy and apparently, I was, but I wasn't sure why? I didn't think much of death apart from the food.

I recovered to my position and Mammy leaned over and gave me a reassuring nip. Now that was sore. I was slowly coming to terms with the protocol.

I am probably the only Christian to have laughed during the rosary at his Grandad's wake. My relations on my mother's side have always held it against me. Not that they were too religious themselves. When we got out of the spare room and the gloom of death – they were mad for billyo. Jokes, yarns and good ones were on the menu all night – even not so funny stories were elevated to great ones. An abbreviated, paraphrased, melodramatic version of John Maguire's life was stuffed down our gullets along with chicken dinner, a meat tea and all the sandwiches you could get your leg over.

My Grandad wasn't dealt the best of hands, he had a tough life. He hid his pain behind a camouflage of good speaks and jollity, but he was always a visitor. He would have made a great family man, but that honour was taken from him and now he was in the spare room getting laid out and ready for his best trip ever – or so we were told.

Geraldine was never a show off – but they all thought she was fierce cute that evening. I sat in the corner with the big sow's head on me. I sucked my thumb and sulked. I always used the dirty towel hanging by the range as my comfort. It was only alright when it was clean, but hypnotic when it had spent a week drying dirty hands and feet – these were the smells of home and family and comfort – we were a clatty lot and this towel stank of us and I clung to it. Of course, I was a big seven and a huge embarrassment to everyone. My mother had gone to great lengths to get me off sucking the thumb. She persuaded the Auld Lad to buy English Mustard in Kate Dolan's shop – the only thing he ever bought there, apart from the paper. She smeared it on my thumb – reminded me of where it came from and waited. I didn't like mustard and I was well aware of its shady past with the rats and the cats piss, but I wouldn't be prized away from my primitive suckling. I licked the mustard off like it was cream and continued till I was really big and in long trousers.

If Grandad's death hadn't sunk in – then this constant feeding and feasting on nice things was really starting to take its toll. Who was I? This carry-on was so alien, I began to worry that our identity had been taken away – but not for long. There was the funeral and Granny came and the ones from Manorhamilton – Daddy's crowd. They came over to the house after and had a small tea and left very respectfully and thankfully – before Mammy's crowd came back from the pub. And there was one last big hooly, where shirts were opened and characters were stripped and laid bare for all to see. A shocking display of carelessness and joy – just what Grandad would have wanted. The day after that melee of gleeful misbehavior, our world and our dietary intake came crashing back to normal. You'd think there'd have been something left over, but there wasn't – not a slice of ham, a wishbone or a pickle – not a biscuit or a slice of sweet cake – no beer, no tears, even the mustard was gone.

We were firmly back to normal and I was glad. I didn't like seeing my Mam and Dad in their good clothes all the time. It felt like they were neglecting their obligation towards us. Now it was just us – the six of us. Daddy was forty-four – Mammy was twenty-nine – Margaret ten – Kevin nine – I was six and Geraldine was three. The next one to leave would be Margaret when she was seventeen. So, seven years of the six of us was coming up. Time to start thinking about some home improvements.

Most ones at school had a bathroom – Tomás Mimna had a bathroom – it was 1972 – everyone on the telly had a bathroom, that we could make out. Our telly was fuzzy and not up to scratch – we had to go to Mimna's to watch the All-Ireland that year. Yes, it was time to knock a hole in the wall of the kitchen – another doorway to – maybe a bathroom? And maybe not!

CHAPTER 16

Bogged Down

My father cut hair – I had the worst haircut in our school. It's now called the pudding bowl hair cut – back then it was normal. Mine was particularly normal. They told me it was to do with the shape of my head and the texture of my hair. My head was round and my hair was soft and straight. It didn't matter what way it was combed, not that it was combed too often, but it just fell back down and I looked like a big thick child. I was bigger than most, so I looked an even bigger thick.

My father was a handy man – not highly skilled at anything in particular – just had good hands on him. He had an uncommon and unlikely confidence when it came to tackling a bit of carpentry or building or electrical wiring. New methods and gadgets didn't faze him – he explored and experimented with care and patience. Sometimes these ventures didn't turn out as expected – sometimes there was a spark or a leak or a drop of blood spilt, but nobody knew any different.

My father remained the go-to man for wiring sockets, hooking up drinkers and cutting hair. He cut the McCaffery's hair. Pat had a great head of hair – Eugene had less hair, but more head – and took just as long. Young Oliver Reilly from Toome was another survivor – obviously hair fashion wasn't on his agenda. There were others too – you'd see them all at Mass on Sundays – whole sections of ones with the same haircut. The Auld Fella could look up the chapel and spot a lad who had gone a bit wispy. He'd tell him to call over during the week. No money passed hands, he just thought he was good at it and wanted to share his gift. He had a great expression when the odd hair-do went askew – *"Millions will never see it"*. And he was right.

It was the early summer of '73 – the turf was on the bank and waiting above in Drumshangore Bog. The bog was a few hundred yards up the road – just past Tom Mimna's and before Toome Lane. Every summer, the bog was a hive of activity. The Reillys, the Pattersons, the Murrays, Pat Fitz, the Mimnas, the Corbys and loads more. Everyone had a turf-bank. Everyone had a Jim Rourke haircut. The turf-banks were stripped and men cut deep into the bog – sometimes fifteen foot deep. In our part of the country the turf would be cut with a breast-spade – a flat rectangular spade with an edge on three sides. The cutter fired them up and they were caught by the catcher standing on the bank. They'd be put on the flat-bed of a wooden turf-barrow and wheeled out to a wider area where they would be tossed. The catcher always under pressure to get back into position without disrupting the rhythm of the cutter.

My father was always the cutter. Mammy would catch and wheel or some of us when we were big enough. When the initial cutting was done, the turf had to be spread, if there was time – sometimes there was no time. Then Mammy would take a fit some Saturday and gather us all up and head for the bog. The turf would be carefully placed around the heathery bank and left to dry. If the weather came good – they'd be turned; if it stayed good – they'd be lifted and put into towers; more fine weather – the turf would be clamped and then finally brought home. A good clamp of turf would keep a fire going for a month. When country people reflect and say they spent the summer in the bog – they are not exaggerating. Lots of summers were not so good, weather-wise and the operation got dragged out even longer.

The bog was an adventure park. Trails and walkways and bog holes. Bog holes – full of bog water. You never knew whether a hole was one foot deep or twenty feet deep. Our mother always shouting, *"Stay away from them bog holes"*, and we mostly did.

On the 8th of May – the day before Geraldine's fifth birthday, we were brought out to the bog to spread turf. Daddy seldom did this, because of his extremely long legs, which left him a long way from the ground. It was only years later we realised that he also had long arms - and if he had bent over, he could have lifted and spread turf just the same as anyone else. Margaret was left at home that day to get the tea ready. These outings were all about work, but you could head off out through the bog exploring, if you had to go for a piddle. I was always ready with a piddle and so the adventure began.

I was gone for a while; Mammy was keeping an eye on Geraldine, and Kevin was beavering away as usual. Then Kevin was told to stop working. He did. My mother called out my name – there was no reply. She repeated it and said she would not be repeating it again – but she did – lots of times. There was still no reply. She flew into a panic – told Kevin to mind his sister and she went darting from one bog hole to the next.

The bog is a very quiet place – not the same birdsong as you'd hear elsewhere. There's lots of dragonflies there and frogs, but mostly quiet. This day – the quiet was horrid quiet. Then she saw it – a perfect circle of blond hair floating in a bog hole. She feared the worst – the sun glistened on the water – funny what nature offers when you're at your most vulnerable. She grabbed a fistful of the soft blond hair and pulled. My mother was as strong as an ox. The only woman I ever saw muscles on, till 'Wonder Woman' came on the telly a few years later.

I was fired out onto the bank like a wet sod of turf. The impact dislodging a lung full of bog water and I started spluttering and she started naming saints. She often brought them up in times of terror or great joy. This was both. I nearly got a hug that day. I was told not to get lost again or fall into a bog hole and then we were all gathered up and marched down the road.

I've never been a fan of water. We grew up surrounded by lakes and rivers and few of us learned to swim. I was nearly drowned on three separate occasions at different stages in my life and each time I was in the water. The Auld Fella always said, *"Can ya not stay away from water, if you can't swim?"*.

Margaret didn't have the tea ready when we got home – we were early and she was caught listening to radio Luxembourg. Mammy didn't even say to turn it off. She brought me upstairs and got me out of my wet clothes. I took off my lovely shirt that Aunt Peggy gave me. The one with the dancing Spanish ladies and their umbrellas. I was shivering and probably in shock. She found clean clothes that fitted and socks without holes – that's Mammies for ya – I could never find clean stuff that didn't need a stitch. She said it was because I never opened my eyes wide enough. Then, I nearly got another hug, but instead, Mammy looked around the room, tutted and started tidying. She told me to sit up on the bed and she got to work.

My mother was at her best when she was working – she fired every stitch of clothes me and Kevin had, out on the floor and started sorting – 'Nights in White Satin' played on the radio below us - my two sisters sang along. This wasn't sweet serenity, but it was as close as I was going to get in Drumshangore. Every bird has their own song.

Kevin came to the top of the stairs to see if I was I alright and would he go to the well? *"Oh Jesus, stay away from the well"*, was my mother's reply – and then,

"Aye, maybe go to the well, but don't fall in... tell some of them ones down there to fill the tank, I'm going to put on a wash".

It might sound a little over-dramatic to say that Mammy's words were greeted with stunned silence – but they were. Not the filling of the tank – that was a thankless task, but nothing compared to the tail end of her statement – *"I'm going to put on a wash"*. These words filled the house with dread. The radio was switched off – flashing images of washes past started going through our heads. The Monster was about to awake.

For years – no – generations – no – since time began – washing had been done by hand in our house. And then Joe Bunn's sister was having an auction. All her belongings were being sold. Not only that, anyone else who had belongings to sell would bring them to the auction too. Daddy loved auctions, because they were social gatherings and he loved rooting through farm machinery and furniture and tools. This was a big auction, which took place over two nights. The Auld Lad came back the first night fairly excited. There was a washing machine for sale, but as always in our case, there was a snag. It was an American washing machine, much the same size as our 'twenty' tractor – that wasn't the only snag – of course it wasn't. American electrical appliances worked off 120 volts – Irish off 220 – we didn't know what that meant at the time, but the Auld Lad said he knew and the good news was, that there was a transformer coming with the washing machine, a yoke almost as big as itself, that transformed our power to theirs. The not-so-good news, was that this washing machine was part of a set, that included a clothes iron, a soldering iron, a toaster and a drill – some, but not all laundry related.

We had the closest thing to a family meeting the next morning – what did we think? Well, it was a good bit of money and we weren't sure if it worked and we didn't do that much soldering – but it would be great for Mammy. The Auld Lad got out the ruler to measure the scullery and then the biggest event out from the moon-landing and getting the telly was upon us. That evening he went off on the tractor and trailer, with a little extra aftershave and bought the big American washing machine... and the clothes iron and the soldering iron, the toaster and the drill... and the big transformer. When we got up the next morning, the machine was on the back street – he couldn't get it into the scullery – not on his own.

The merchandise was not quite as impressive as Daddy had made it out to be – we reluctantly shifted the main machine off the backstreet into its position. This thing was in a totally different weight division to Mammy – yet many bouts would ensue. It took the Auld Man a while to figure out the electrical configuration and then one free Saturday, we went for it. It was a top loading single tub automatic – we ignored the automatic – filled it from the tank – threw in whatever clothes we weren't wearing at the time and cranked her up. This mother and father of all domestic appliances with its magically transformed voltages and nuclear dashboard switches hummed and dawdled – it would be some time before it decided whether to operate as directed or to completely act the buck. It was a sleeping giant and we were filled with excitement. When it eventually clicked into action, it roared and swayed and pranced and pinned Mammy into the corner of the scullery. It's lid was sometimes 'live' to the touch and when it spun, it took off out the door again.

Mammy loved it – for the first time she didn't have to wash clothes by hand. It stayed fairly close to the house for over ten years, until one day near Christmas, it ate three of Daddy's shirts, a pair of drawers and two tea-towels and suddenly drowned in its own soapy water. The drill, the clothes iron, the soldering iron and the eight-slice toaster were never the same after.

That day, when I nearly drowned – Mammy sorted our room – she gathered up my wet clothes – and the dirty ones – she grabbed my circular hair once more and smiled. She said, *"Do ya know, you nearly drowned and what would we do then?"*.   There's no answer for that and she didn't want one. It was time for another rumble in the Scullery.

The next day, we were back in the bog, all of us. Daddy brought a pitchfork to use instead of stooping, Mammy did the most work as usual, but we all helped. Our zest for adventure somewhat quenched from the day before. We had tea on the bank – two bottles of tea – wrapped in towels. Big slices of batch loaf with butter and corned beef and an apple cake. It didn't get much better than this.

But we wanted more. Time to quiz the Auld Lad about the telly – ones at school had stations other than RTE – when could we get the BBC or UTV? When could we get colour? What about the bathroom project – when was that going to reopen? After tea, we walked over to a wee gorge at the bottom of the pass, a place we were fascinated with. It was where people dumped stuff at the time; a load of household rubbish – glistening like treasure in the afternoon sun. Stuff that we wouldn't throw out if we had it, but we weren't allowed take anything home in case we'd be found stealing from the dump. Stealing from other people's lives when we had enough to be going on with ourselves.

Then it was time to stop the dreaming and thicken into our work. The evening ahead not as attractive – now that tea-time was over – but in the distance there was hope. Clouds – dark clouds and rumblings of thunder. God was coming to our rescue. Suddenly a shower of the straightest rain you could ever wish for came pelting down out of the sky – sent turf-mold zinging into the air. We were soaked in seconds. We hurriedly gathered up the picnic and the tools and made a run for it. I knew what it was like to be heading home from the bog – soaked. Now, we all did.

CHAPTER 17

Medals and Sweets

Mammy and Daddy were gone to town to buy togs and cement and a dicky-bow – if they could find a dicky-bow. Mammy rarely went shopping with Daddy – unless there was something he could get wrong – togs or dicky-bows were not his thing. The cement was for the new bathroom. We weren't going to build a bathroom just yet, but we were going to tidy up the 'World War II' type hole in the back wall of the house. *"It's a scandal"*, Mammy would say – of course, she didn't really mean that – she just thought if she said it often enough – the Auld Man might be shamed into action – and he was. He was going to get cement and a doorframe and a door and put the doorframe in the hole and patch around it and then nail the door into the doorframe and hope that Mammy would keep quiet – and she did.

The bathroom project would be no further on – in fact, this latest action meant that it was over – he had another plan – a more long-term plan. Somewhere inside his brain was the nucleus of an idea. This would be the boldest yet and it would take the most of ten years to complete. He was thinking of building a new house.

More imminently, I needed a dicky-bow. I was about to get my first Holy Communion and while everyone else was being adorned in the fashion hives of Ballinamore and Killashandra. I was short only one thing – a dicky-bow. I had fairly good shoes, that would come up just fine with a bit of spit and polish. I had very good short trousers and newish underpants. I had a lovely yellow shirt that I fell into the bog-hole with and Mammy had knitted the loveliest mustard coloured cardigan. All I needed was a dickie-bow.

I hated what I was going to be wearing. I had put the outfit on a few times to show Mammy, as she thought it was lovely or I was lovely and when I looked in the mirror, I saw me and the state of me and that's not what I wanted to see.

There was a lot of talk about this Communion at school – it was like a hole in the fence and if you couldn't get through it, you were going to miss out on all the advantages of being a good Catholic. I wasn't too put out by that, because I couldn't think of anyone who had failed to proceed beyond Communion.

Maybe it's because Mammy was always knitting, but I didn't like knitted things. There was always wool to be rolled or held – always loads of *"Arms up – arms apart"* and *'Hold it… hold it – hold it up and out…!".* Our concentration levels never matched Mammy's. I was frumpy enough without wool. The knitted football socks were a nice touch when I was younger and more naïve – but even them and the subsequent knitted football shorts proved fairly impractical when it rained. I had worn the woollen ensemble to a match in Aughnasheelin and as the game progressed, I was finding more air around my nether regions, because the stitches were stretching with the movement and I didn't have anything else under them – then there came a shower of rain and that was it. My socks peeled down over my 'Blackthorn' boots and my togs soaked up the moisture and headed for the cavity of my backside – also, my tiddler and appendages were shifted to one side – as a sort of backways thong took shape. My skill-set reduced to keeping certain parts covered, while gainfully trying to play my way back into the game. Wool was no longer my friend – not in a sock – not in a reliable hold-all for my privates and now as a tan/brown first Holy Communion cardigan, it disappointed. Tomás Mimna would have a nice blazer and long trousers – the Lees wouldn't be great, but at least they'd be respectable – Catriona O'Kelly would look like an angel in her outfit and I looked like a coughed-up fur-ball.

The third item on the shopping list was the most important – proper football togs – since the knitted ones disappeared up the Khyber – I had played in my short trousers and played well – well, at least – I was hands free, but the new togs were for my debut in the 'Drumreilly Sports Day' – an annual event loosely based on athletics that took place in Quinn's fairly flat field near Drumcoura. There was running and jumping and throwing and if you were middling big, you had a good chance of winning a medal. I was a horrid size for my age and so had high hopes of a winning start to my athletic career.

There were no togs in Ballinamore that would fit me. The Auld Pair got the cement and the dicky-bow and a lamp-shade for the parlour that no one ever used, but no togs. I played hurt – very hurt – and the Auld Fella was sent to Killashandra for togs the following Saturday – the day of the sports. It was one o'clock and he still wasn't back. No togs, no lift and no money to get in. Me, Margaret and Kevin started off walking. The sports were at three and it was a good hour away. We walked up the road, past Hyland's shop and into the heart of Drumreilly. Past Drumlea Chapel and then on our left, 'Holahan's Bottom' – this was Drumreilly's football field – often referred to as, 'The White Man's Graveyard'. Some of the best footballers in Connacht played in this bit of bottom ground – some of the greatest acts of terror took place there too. From a young age we were warned not to be caught gawking in, as it was a sign of weakness to show any interest. We couldn't help pick out the bare patch where 'The Red Fella' levelled one of the Aughavas's with a box – the sound of his jaw breaking could be heard on Corrawallen bog and some of his teeth were turned up by a hay tedder the following year.

By the time we got to Quinn's field – the haze had lifted and it was now sunny and warm. There was a sight of cars parked along the road. The Drumreilly's were great for supporting their own. A sports day in Carrigallen would be a disaster because no one would go – everyone otherwise engaged – everyone a notch above running and jumping for no reason. In Drumreilly they loved it and all were welcome – at least anyone with 5p.

There was a caravan in the middle of the field with loud speakers and they were calling the boys under 8's – I was under 8 and I was outside and I had no togs and no 5p and I was just about to piddle on myself when our dear lovely headmaster, Tommy Moran came along and said they were calling my race. He paid for me to get in and what's more, he vouched for my age. The Drumreilly's said I looked more like seventeen than seven, but I was lined up at the start and for the first time, I was about to race against someone other than my brother.

I whipped off my shoes and the whistle blew. I was in front from the start – twice the size of the others – and no one was going to catch me. It's the strangest feeling being at the front – it didn't happen often in my life – but there's no feeling like charging for the line and knowing you're going to win. It's ironic really, that my first medal would be for what I was least good at – running fast. My first race, my first medal and I couldn't find my brother and sister. They were still on the road with no money and no sign of Daddy. Kevin decided to break in through a hedge and he did. Margaret decided to wait and then Daddy came with that smile he used to have after a few bottles of beer. He brought togs and money for sweets and the day couldn't get much better – but it did.

There was another race – the under 10's – I put on my new, faster running togs for that and I won and I went to the caravan and I got two gold medals and I hung around with the Auld Fella, just in case my age was questioned again. I had won my first two races – one with togs – one without. People were saying hello to the Auld Lad and then saying, *"This must be your young fella, he's the spit of ya"* and then I'd show them my medals.

People are always impressed with medals – you can't argue with medals. That day in Quinn's field, I outran everyone under the age of ten. I thought I was an athlete. I sort of was, but I might have peaked too soon. Still, my first experience in individual competitive sport was positive and that's when I decided I was going to be a sportsman and a footballer and a much sought-after personality.

We met Tom Mimna that day after – and Tomás. Tom was a first cousin of Daddy's, but also a great friend and neighbour. He was in his fifties now and a heavy set – he smoked eighty cigarettes a day and had a bad chest. He was also a fine cross-country runner in his time. With little or no training, he had won Ulster titles with 'The Tom Regan Harriers' – an athletic club based in Belturbet, County Cavan. My father reminded me of this – several times. His way of keeping me grounded. He also pointed out Pat Conefrey, a former County footballer with Leitrim, when Leitrim were at their best. I caught a glimpse of a young Frank Holahan there too. He would go on to be one of Leitrim's greatest footballers. There was something about the way he moved – with such ease and grace. Drumreilly had lots of warriors – men who had danced with success and fame. Men who had pitted themselves against the best and found out their worth. That's what attracted me to sport. What's inside you when you're pushed to the limit by the best?

I had just run through the rushes and the cow tracks to beat off a few malnourished Drumreilly childer and I was thinking in tones of All-Ireland and Olympic glory. Time to put back on me short trousers and go for sweets. Daddy would surely stop at Hyland's on the way home – to show them my medals – and he did. We got ice-cream – a block of ice-cream and wafers. When we got home, Mammy, with the precision of a seamstress, divided the block into six. Four equals and two slivers for her and my old man. Mammy and Daddy eating ice-cream was the funniest thing.

CHAPTER 18

Holy Moly

The night before my First Holy Communion, I slept in a hair-net. There wasn't one bit need for me to sleep in a hair-net – me with the most predictable hair in three provinces. But Mammy said I had to sleep on my back with my arms by my side, in a hair-net in case I'd ruffle my extremely clean; round; soft; straight hair. That was Mammy's way of saying, this is a very important day – don't mess it up on everyone! I hated my hair and my head and this make-shift outfit hanging on the end of the wardrobe. What's more – I hated the wardrobe and the peeling wallpaper with the black streaks of tar coming down the chimney breast and I hated St Patrick in his sandals looking down on me, all disappointed. He was lucky he wasn't taken off the wall that morning and shoved out the window where we emptied the pots! This was not going to be the kind of day that normal youngsters look forward to.

I'm sure the Lees and the Kellys and the Lynchs were in their bathrooms – looking into a mirror and full of the joys of their youth. I bet Tomás Mimna's Aunty Maggie had just stopped off with a train-set or even more Lego or marbles or a Communion rosette – they were big back then – like what you'd put on a horse, but at least it was some bit of glamour. I had wet the bed and is it any wonder and the pressure I was under. I smelt of piss, but at least my hair was straight. This bloody house and this bloody family.

Kevin had a hair-net too – he looked like a girl – and my brother was the furthest thing from a girl. He was my role-model and there he was in the bed beside me looking like I had slept with Joe Bunn's mother. But at least he'd be going to my Communion in long trousers and yes, he had a cardigan too, but Kevin was thin, he could wear wool. He could have worn both cardigans and he'd still look okay. Why did I have to carry all the weight of the family? Mammy was shouting up at us to get up. We had to get up and help do the things – even today – especially today – because we'd have to be ready to go to Mass early and not be trapesing up through the chapel and Mass on and the state of me.

Normally, Mammy'd be outside when we got up, but this morning, she was downstairs waiting to see how we looked. She wouldn't let us take off the nets until we were ready to go to Mass – otherwise, we'd probably get our hair caught in something. Now it would have to be covered completely for doing the things, in case it got splattered by a cows tail or a dunt of a calf. We could have worn hats, but she decided to put plastic bags over our netted noggins instead.

Nowhere else in the world would this take place. A dig into our dignity and a slur on our standing is what it was. Kevin was, as always, agreeable and headed off like a bald eagle to bring in the cows. I too, had to abide. I offered it up to St Jude – the patron saint of hopeless cases.

The morning felt quite surreal as we did our jobs. I felt like I was preparing for something big, but nobody was telling me what it was. I knew about the Holy Spirit and the body of Christ and all that – and I was sorry for telling lies at my first confession, but what was I supposed to do? I didn't have any sins of my own. I was an eight-year-old from south Leitrim in 1973 – sins were like hen's teeth back then. Today was just going to be one embarrassing situation after another, enough to piddle on yourself with shame.

God wasn't as religious as some of the ones down our way. But the mix of religion and my family never really worked. I'm not sure if they really bought into it. We always went to Mass. We never took part though. Oh, we went up for Communion and we stood up and sat down and whatever was going on around us, but we never really listened to what the priest was saying. When the priest came to the house, it was just a case of keeping him at bay till he left. No one talked to him – Daddy ummed and ahhhh'd and Mammy pumped him full of tea and sponge cake that she had kept from us. I know it was me who laughed when Grandad died, but you should have seen the faces of them. No one was thinking of Grandad and that he was in a better place, that he had found peace – they were all thinking the same as me – *'Why did we paint these walls purple?'* Was it for sorrow?

Things went smooth enough around the byre and sheds that morning. Herself was very focused and Daddy was on his toes. He wasn't always on his toes, but the look of determination on my mother's face that morning would frighten the life out of a bishop. I had another 'cat's-lick' of a wash after the milking and I took off the bag and the hair-net. My hair looked exactly like it did every other morning, but now my head was redder than usual – from the pressure. I looked like I had been hung up-side-down overnight – like a turkey at Christmas. I kept hoping that maybe the outfit might strike a new look on the day – but it looked and felt as it had when I tried it on previously. I was just going to have to accept that it was punishment for everything bad that I had done and was about to do. *'Just don't piddle in your trousers'* is all I thought as we headed off.

Geraldine looked cute, as usual – Kevin was committed, as usual. Margaret on the other hand, no more than myself, had to endure some desperate fashion misjudgements. She always looked like she had been hung up-side-down. She gave me some solace. We were late. Everyone was there and sitting in their seats and then we came in, tramping up through the chapel, like the only family who were told to come in fancy dress. I could have killed God that morning. Was there any need for this humiliation? Poor Margaret was nearly thirteen and about to get Confirmation and it was her last year at National School and she had grown nine inches since she last wore the dress that she was made to wear. Her hair was as red as her face and we had used up all the hair-nets. Still, she gave me a wink, as much as to say, *"You're not exactly page three of 'The Good Catholic' yourself – Pudgy Face"*. I went all the way to the front and they sat in the cheap seats. Thankfully, this was as bad as it got.

A woman I didn't know came creeping from the Drumbrick side of the chapel and pushed something into my hand. It was a whole 50p. I looked at Mammy and she beckoned me to turn around and sit up straight and not be looking like a big thick overgrown child in short trousers and a tan/brown/mustard/orange cardigan. I looked to Margaret and she winked – again. A, *'Now ya boy ya'* sort of wink. There was money to be made looking like this. I didn't know that. I looked around to see if there was anyone else I didn't know. A small man was sent over by his wife, and he gave me 40p and said, *"You'll play for Drumreilly"* – I thought – I might have, if you had given me fifty.

I might have had the worst short trousers in the place, but they had the biggest, deepest pockets and I was taking in money, left, right and centre. I was very disappointed when Mass kicked off, as that put an end to the gifts. It was a lovely Mass, now that I had found my true faith. Singing, praying and my first taste of the blessed holy bread – the Communion itself – the body of Christ – he could have done with a bit more flavour, but that was it. A few more prayers and Mass was over – go forth in peace. Amen.

If the few shillings before Mass surprised me – then I had no idea to the extent of what was to come. Auld ones breaking their backs to get giving me money. I was where I wanted to be – the centre of attention – and for all the right reasons. There were group photographs and then there was a photograph of me and my mate Tomás.

My family didn't take any photos, because we didn't have a camera. There was never a camera in our house, till Geraldine bought one years and years later. My father had this thing about cameras – don't know what it was. He himself was very photogenic, but till the day he died, he never took a photograph. When he and my mother were twenty-five years married – we sent them on a trip around Ireland and we also sent with them a disposable camera, which were all the go at the time. You could take twenty-five photos and my mother did. When they came back the camera was full. It was only when the photographs were developed, that we realised she had been holding the camera the wrong way round.

My Uncle Michael would come home from New York every year and say, *"Why don't you get a camera, it would be nice to record the passing years!"*. My father would fly into his camera speech. *"I don't have a camera, I never had a camera, I have no need for a camera – and so I won't be getting one any time soon"*. We stopped mentioning it, but I often wondered why he reacted like he did.

I think he was aware of the fragility of our lives. He was very aware that this world we had created for ourselves – and which he had huge responsibilities for –mightn't hold up to any great amount of scrutiny. Why capture a moment that will only show up the short-comings of our lives and personalities? Maybe it might be better to carry on unknowing. Never looking back – never standing still and never asking why. It's not that he thought he had failed in any way – just that there was no point gazing at something we couldn't change. I agree. I used to think that a camera – in the hands of an amateur – doesn't captures the essence of what is truly happening, but perhaps I'm wrong. Maybe those old photos are too close to the bone. Maybe they capture exactly what was going on.

CHAPTER 19

Thinning Out

By the time I was eleven, I could get into the Guards, I was that big. I could hardly walk from pains in me knees; my joints not able to take the sudden change in my body. I remember having to reverse up the steps to Drumeela chapel, as it was the only way I could master it. *"You'll have them pains"*, I was told. *"That's what you get for growing so quick"*. I also had a constant headache. In hindsight, it was probably sinus, but we seldom went to doctors and I didn't mention it. I was also mad into football at this stage and was starting to miss out because of my knees. That's when I decided to do something about it.

With the lack of professional help, I self-diagnosed that I was too heavy and needed to become thin and then all my pains would be gone. So, I stopped eating. I had porridge in the morning and the smallest dinner I could get away with, and I dreamed of getting thin – and I did. The fact that it coincided with the greatest growth spurt known to man, probably accentuated it. They were getting worried about me at home – that was a good sign. I was also getting ready to leave Drumeela National School and head for the Tech in Carrigallen. I had my Confirmation in May of '76 – another high fashion moment in the O'Rourke household.

Well in fact, this time I got my way. I wore the widest bell-bottom trousers imaginable – platform shoes – another yellow shirt with print and a tweed jacket. Of course, I still had the hair – thicker and longer and even more perfectly round. I looked like a giant rivet.

But I now had all the sacraments and I was finished National School and ready for LIFE. I was only gone eleven, so I must have skipped classes at school – they did that if you were too big for a class – they'd move you up one, so you didn't stand out as being too stupid. I was neither stupid or clever, just relieved to be done. School wasn't that bad – but it had been nearly seven years of my life that I hadn't fully committed to. Seven years of rhyming off and joining in. Seven years in which I learned to act.

We didn't do acting classes – drama was not a subject in Drumeela – but we had a teacher who did facilitate our acting out. Stories were made and we acted the parts. I started off in non-speaking roles – some non-moving roles. I was very effective as a door and a standing shelf – and I quickly latched on to the idea of acting and being someone else. I also learned that I could have more impact on my audience by doing less. What I was really trying to do, was annoy Tommy Moran – just because he was the teacher and he looked like he could take it. It was all very simple, but totally unrestrained and in there somewhere, I saw the magic – and comfort of role playing. It would be more than ten years until I'd use that skill publicly, but it was in there somewhere.

Now though, I wanted to be a footballer like Frank Holahan or Noel Maxwell from Drumreilly – or Micky Martin from Carrick. The Leitrim Under 21 team had won the Connacht Championship in '75 and just lost out to Kerry in the All-Ireland Semi-Final the same year. The match was in Carrick-on-Shannon. Me and Kevin had dragged our father off to the game one drizzly Saturday. As fond as he was of football – the Auld Lad didn't like getting wet. Also, it wasn't a natural direction for us to go to watch football. We had grown up with Cavan football – we'd be in Breffni Park every second Sunday. We went to Ulster matches in Clones. Going to Carrick was unfamiliar, but at the same time – it felt very right. This was the game that would spark my interest in being a 'County Man'. I was ten and I loved the way they ran onto the pitch with such intent – like men possessed – gladiators – soldiers – representing us – as they did that day, with such skill and valour. Surely it wouldn't be long before Leitrim would be great. Would they wait for me?

First, I had to get my body right. In the summer of '76 in between Drumeela and the Tech – I was fasting. I could tell by my clothes that I was losing weight. I was shocking hungry, but I was also fierce thick. My mother was getting worried that I might be sick. She thought that I was pale and thin and subdued. That's because I was pale and thin and subdued. And hungry. I said nothing. She said she was going to bring me to Dr Farrelly in Ballinamore, if I didn't improve. I struggled with the idea of telling lies and putting the Auld Pair out the price of a doctor's visit, when I knew exactly what was wrong with me – or in my head – what was right with me. Going to the doctor or calling out the doctor to an old person was one thing – but there was a certain indignity in having a child sick – so people back then were reluctant to fuss. The only other time the doctor was mentioned was when I ate the feed of beetroot and me mother thought I had the Red Water.

In July we were at the hay. The usual panic between the showers to try and get hay ready for cocking. Everyone in the meadow – turning; tedding; wondering; looking up at the sky and hoping. The Auld Pair hoping it would stay dry – some other members of the family, hoping that the heavens would open. That evening, I got my wish. A big plosh of rain coming up to three o'clock. My mother said that was it – she was bringing me to Dr Farrelly. It's not that I was looking particularly thin that day, but it's just with the shower of rain, I would have put on an even more forlorn pout than usual – pretending to be disappointed. Plus, with rain coming they had nothing to do for the evening, apart from go home and wash the street – but the other three were made do that and me and Mammy and the Auld Fella headed into Ballinamore.

Normally, getting off to town with the Auld Pair was a mighty treat, as they could very well stop and get 'foosie' or some sort of sweets, but I was on a diet and I wouldn't be eating anything like that. There was also the danger of being found out. I knew from my acting experience at Drumeela, that less was more. It was important to be sick for this man. Doctors expect sickness and I was going to give him – dull; sunken; withdrawn; hopeless; inward pain. And I did.

My father sat in the car – he had to drive, because Mammy couldn't drive, but that's all he had to do. Women were better with doctors. Better at explaining – how could a man explain what was going on with his son without it seeming like a flaw in himself. No, Daddy sat this one out.

Dr Farrelly was a wily man – fond of a drop – was probably a better actor than me and had years of experience in dealing with worried mothers. He was stout and cheerful and hard not to like.

"Well, what could be the matter with this fine man?"

"Do you not think he's very thin, Doctor?"

"Compared to what? Not as thin as Mulvaney's goat"

"He's very pale and thin, Doctor"

"Is he eating?"

"His appetite is gone"

"Where did it go to, I wonder"

Dr Farrelly wasn't one bit worried about me – said I was probably starting to chase girls and there's nothing to knock the weight off, like a fast woman. He couldn't prescribe any medicine – but a bet-up egg in the morning might do the trick – a tonic – to get my strength up for the up-coming romance in my life. He stood back and smiled and said, *"Does he talk?"*. My mother said with great pride, *"Not much, the same fella"*. *"I wonder if he talked, what would he say?"*. Dr Farrelly seemed more worried about my silence than my thinning jaw.

"Try eating a bit, young Rourke, or you'll never play for Leitrim". He hit the nail on the head and suddenly, he could see the light in my eyes. It was only then he relaxed, content that he had struck a chord. He went to the door – opened it and said. *"Bring that man down the town Mrs Rourke and get him chips"*. Dr Farrelly wouldn't take money. He squeezed the crumpled-up pound note in my mother's hand and said, *"Keep it for the chips"*. He winked and smiled and went to his desk.

There were few heroes in our lives at the time – Muhammad Ali; because he was 'The Greatest' – Fr Patsy Young; because he brought the Mart to Carrigallen and Doctor Farrelly of Ballinamore. We stopped at the chipper. The Auld Lad wouldn't eat chips – thought it was an awful thing to be doing to good potatoes and us with a field full of them at home. But I had chips and Mammy had one or two – she didn't like eating them in front of himself. We brought chips home to the others and there was a sight of water drank that evening.

As the summer progressed, I had my bet-up egg every morning. Two raw eggs – two spoons of sugar – a drop of milk and whisk. I sat in a bit closer to the table and gradually my limbs and my joints and my head came together in a truce. I practiced my football every chance I got, I used the meadow and the bog as my gym and I ran everywhere. I would never have speed, but I could carry two buckets of water from the well, as quick as anybody. I was taller than my mother and my sisters, I was nearly as tall as my brother and all was well.

We watched the All-Ireland Football Final that year, in Tom Mimna's – they had a colour television. Dublin won back their title from Kerry. It was a golden age for football. The country people supporting Kerry, I was secretly supporting the Dubs, because of the glamour they brought and because of Brian Mullins – their towering midfielder. He was tall and mean and played the game like his life depended on it. At that moment in time, my life did depend on football. It was all I had.

CHAPTER 20

Holding On

In September '76 – it was time to start the Tech in Carrigallen. I was no longer a child. I wasn't sure about the academic side of this new school – but I was ready for any amount of acting the jinnet. I was about to let loose – like our suck calves when we'd let them into the field in front of the house – I was going to kick up my heels and knock down any obstacle or small teacher that got in my way. I was a runaway train, but first I had to get the bus.

Dessie Patterson drove the yellow school bus, slow. We were always late – Margaret and Kevin and now me. We would be picked up at Clogher Cross in the morning and then dropped off at the bottom of the lane in the evening. It was called the monkey bus – it collected and dropped off monkeys along the route through Aughavas, Corrawallen, Newtowngore, Doogra, Doogarry – up the mountain and back the bog road by Drumeela into Carrigallen. That hour on the bus in the morning was pure hardship, once we got in on the swing of how to misbehave.

Dessie was the mildest, most good-humoured man you could ask to drive this vintage crock and we all helped. When he used the bus for bringing suck-calves to the new cattle mart, which was on our way, he had lots of budding farmers to sit up front and help with the nervous animals. That wasn't my scene. I was more into horseplay. Shoving, pushing, 'holding the back seat' – playing hardy knuckles – hardy chests – school-bag fights and wrestling. That's when I got over the shock of this new school. For now, though – my first morning – heading off to big school was dangerous, because I had never been on a bus before.

I was told to 'mind':

> *"Mind, do ya hear? Mind getting on the bus – and off... wait till it stops... sit in your seat... don't eat your lunch till you get to school... don't be annoying Dessie Patterson... keep your schoolbag on your knee or between your legs and don't be acting the maggot".*

To be honest, I was more conscious of my 'Farah' trousers – which had been my good trousers, until they got too short and Mammy let them down an inch, when it was too late and now they were just above my ankles and very hugging around my thighs. I had shocking big thighs for a boy. There was no school uniform in those days – the cool lads from around the mountain had denim jeans and denim shirts with badges sewn on – Rock, was their God – heavy metal – 'Status Quo' – 'Led

Zeppelin' – 'Motor Head' – I hadn't a clue. We had just got our first tape recorder to tape stuff off the radio. The first pre-recorded tape we got was 'Brendan Shine' – I wasn't going to mention that.

I have to admit, I was numb. This often happened at times of change. I'd get hit with a sudden bout of melancholy. A fear that I was taking a step forward with unfinished business left behind. Was that it? Was that childhood? A few bits of Lego and a leather ball – standing in gaps and tedding hay? Mindin' we didn't fall into the well or get drowned in a bog-hole. I was no philosopher, but I had my doubts about the place and environment I was growing up in. I was eleven and a half and all I heard from I was a baby, was: *"It's well for some – enjoy your childhood – it won't last forever – school days are the best days of your life!"* Did I miss something? The only thing that was keeping me going, was that I might get to play football for Leitrim and maybe drive a lorry.

Robert Mitchell got on the bus somewhere about Doogra – he had the same problem as me – with the trousers – and it didn't look like 'Black Sabbath' were big in his house either. I looked out the window – I was going to keep myself to myself. That's when I got a clatter across the back of the head from Oliver Reilly – I knew him from one of Daddy's haircuts. He was one of the few youngsters who trusted my father or who knew no better. He was in second year and looked like he had just eaten a townland. He challenged me in a site-specific game.

I would hold onto the cross-bar of the seat in front of me and let him beat my hands with his fists until I let go – see how long I could hold on for.

If I had thought as much about this impromptu game as I had about the early life of a Leitrim child, I might have saved myself some pain. But no, I asked no questions – rose to the challenge immediately and grabbed the three-quarter-inch tubular bar that ran across the back of the seat in front of me. Even Oliver was surprised by my stupidity. He smiled, rolled up his sleeves to reveal his very impressive muscular forearms, his huge freckled hands and polished knuckles – and without any warning or, *"When would you like me to start, Seamus?"* – 'Whistling Pat's' youngest son, suddenly and mindlessly began to savagely beat the hands off me with his fists. With the rhythm and precision of a jackhammer, he flailed into me – the bar bending with each thump – my hands were surprised and swelling – his eyes met my eyes – his eyes were sparkling – my eyes were bulging and tearing up and wondering, what the hell is happening and when is it going to stop? That's when I remembered the game. It doesn't stop until I take my hands off – but that would mean giving in – I wasn't going to give in to anything – even if it meant excruciating pain for no reason – this was my chance to prove that I was as thick as I looked – our two Jim Rourke hair-cuts bobbed and danced and my hands were now turning blue.

"Have you had enough young Rourke?"

"No, I'm grand – are you getting tired?"

I shouldn't have said that – I could see the rage build up in this monster from Toome. He sledged down like his reputation depended on it. I began to wonder about my safety. Could this be the moment in my life where I get all my fingers broke? What will I tell them in the hospital? *"I grabbed onto a bar and allowed someone to dis-member my hands"*? I was going to have to ask him to stop – that or take away my hands. It was then I realised that my hands were so pulverized and swollen, that they wouldn't come away from the, by now, flattened tube. Ah well, it wouldn't be too long before we'd arrive at the school and although I may not be able to dip my finger – any finger – into the sugar bowl ever again – this show of stubbornness will surely stand to me somehow.

I could tell Reilly was becoming disillusioned as we reached the Tech. The first-year boys, who had gathered round, were impressed, if a little confused – the first-year girls were uninterested, they fixed themselves and tried to unsee this uncivilized behaviour. I declared victory as we came to a halt at the school gates. No one cared. Oliver Reilly said I was one outrageously thick gossan and walked off. I was left clinging to the seat – not because I wanted to, but because I couldn't let go. Dessie Patterson asked was I alright – said maybe big school mightn't be as bad as I was expecting. I had forgot about school and it being my first day. I made an almighty tug at my hands and released them. It sent a shiver of pain down my arms – I couldn't feel or grip and my schoolbag was gone.

I rushed off the bus almost in tears, only to be met by my brother and sister. Kevin had my bag and his wise eyes said – *"That wasn't a great idea"* – Margaret smiled and said – *"Maybe you should keep your hands in your pockets for a few days"*.

Although the Tech – the Vocational School – was on a hill, it was modest and unassuming – it wasn't put there to impress, but to further educate a rural community that had been shy of further education. It was a place of great honesty and integrity – from it's founders, right up until this present day. It attracted teachers of a practical disposition, with a realistic expectation of its pupils. We all hated school, but few hated the tech. Michael Duignan was the headmaster and was as rough as he was astute. Collectively, he dealt with us by dishing out clatters – haymakers – and yet he had the subtlest of instinct when it came to our individual needs. He cast the funniest aspersions on those equipped to retort and yet had the gentlest of qualities with the delicate of mind – he was the grumpiest, friendliest and proudest of men – he saved us and inspired us – he was decent, yet maligned. At that time he *was* Carrigallen Vocational School. And if Mick Duignan was the stump of the tree – Eamon Daly, the vice principle, was a fresh green shoot – so positive, open and thoughtful. We were blessed to have these and the other seven teachers at the time and boy, did we test them.

We tested them, because we needed to test ourselves – see what we could get away with. It was the first time our personalities would carry any weight – there were changes coming – voices breaking, balls dropping – wee tingling sensations that hadn't bothered us in Drumeela. These next three or four years would point us in a direction – it was time to come out from under our jumpers.

"Look at this Neanderthal coming sloping up the pass" – That's what Mr. Duignan said, when he saw me for the first time. I wasn't the slightest bit put out by the statement as I was three inches taller than I'd been three weeks before – my hands were twice the size of the ones I'd eaten my porridge with that morning and I always walked with a slope, whether climbing a hill or not. Plus, I hadn't a clue what a Neanderthal was. He asked me my name and when I told him, he said, *"Oh good Jesus"*, and walked off. I thought to myself – *'We'll get on just fine'* – it was time to get inside and find somewhere safe to put my lunch and my hands. It was time to start big school.

CHAPTER 21

Let the Saw do the Work

Mammy's homeplace in Druminchingore was now part of our farm. Although it was poor land, it was an extra few acres and it was only down the road. It also had Grandad's three-room cottage and a few outhouses. The Auld Pair came up with a plan to rent out the house for extra revenue. It had no running water, but plans were afoot to connect into a bored well down the lane. There was no bathroom, but that wasn't an issue as lots would take a house without a bathroom in those days. The house had been cleared out shortly after my Grandad died and now needed some attention and a sink. Since I had started the Tech, I had shown an interest in woodwork and metalwork and practical subjects in general – so when it came to this project in Druminchin, I was brought along for my eagerness and my new found height. We had to paint, but also make a press for the sink.

It was late summer and most of the farm work was done. The hay was saved and in and we had the turf home. This was bonus time for a farming family – like we had been given a few extra weeks before the clocks were changed and the weather got scarce. The mood was always different now. There was an extra intake of breath after breakfast and dinner – more squints at the paper – more bread and jam – sups of tea, when it wasn't even tea time. The scramble for time was eased and the days were more spread out. My father was at his best during this short sabbatical from drudgery and gloom. We'd swim in fresher, clearer water for a while. He'd be a different fish from a different school. On days like this, my father took on the persona of a tradesman and so did I. Today, we were carpenters.

The Auld Man hadn't many tools, but made the most of what he had. He had an old handsaw, sharpened and set; a claw hammer; a hand drill and a drawer full of every nail, tack and screw – mostly bent or twisted, but with patience – useful – priceless in my father's eyes. We had a stainless-steel sink, a few lengths of 2x1 timber and 3x2 and two sheets of chipboard. We had to fix and rehang the back door and make a cupboard for under the sink. We had a flask of tea and milk, a box of sandwiches and all day to think and plan and work. We were both in our ally. He'd have thought about this day's work for weeks – the specific jobs and the allotted time for each. His brain worked like mine in that way.

Indeed, it was uncanny how well we worked in unison – our way of thinking just slotted together like a latch on a hook.

One day this house would be the place where I'd live. It has always given me great pride, knowing that it was my Grandfather's house. His family had come here in 1926 from Swanlinbar in West Cavan, on the Fermanagh border. It was originally owned by a man called 'Gordon' and so Grandad's family became known as the 'Gordon Maguires'. It was a four roomed house originally. It was thatched and built with a combination of stone and mud, but in the '60's my Grandfather had knocked the house and rebuilt it – room by room – neglecting to rebuild the last room. The thatch was replaced with slate and instead of mud walls, there was now – not block or stone – but a light concrete mix, poured into badly propped up and tied shuttering. The quaint little house now stood, completely off square and off plumb and infested by woodworm. As crooked as a ram's horn, but the perfect heirloom in more ways than one. Although it was on a hill, it was in a hollow and faced north. In front, a stone shed; behind a shed where poteen was once made; either side – tall fertile chestnut trees. The only light comes in the gate after you and leaves when you go to bed. In it's gardens, haggard and a raised bank to the side, there is magic and intrigue. For years we found bottles, jars and clay pipes, remnants of a vibrant, social hub, where yarns, devilment and poteen flowed. A place where no one's character was safe from ridicule and mockery, where laughter was a valid exchange for lies and exaggerations. This is where made-up people lived and spirits roamed – John Maguire talked of 'Eoin Fafoo' and 'Briardy's Ghost' – There's nothing as spiteful as a dead man's boast.

I had never seen my father as relaxed as today. Some days he gazed beyond those around him – looked for justification in the distance – stretching out a hand to his future self, asking for a pull through. Sometimes he was bored by his limitations and lack of recklessness. Sometimes he longed for something else, but not today. Today he whistled and he hummed, he measured and he cut. I could see his head was free from clutter and chaos and when it was, his contribution was great. He was good company, even for an eleven-year-old half man/half boy.

"Let the saw do the work!" My father handed me the saw – he was waiting for this moment. He had asked me about woodwork class at the Tech – what tools had we? *"That's a sight of tools – can you cut straight?"* I told him I could – he said, *"We'll soon see"*, but that's not when he gave me the saw. He gave me time to think about it, to fret about my first on-site examination. He was a devil like that. Then when he could see I had worked myself into a bit of a state and he had some less important cutting to do – he marked off the end of a good thick 3x2 and he handed me the saw.

"Cut that off, there at the line"
"Will I leave the line"
"Maybe split the line?"

Nothing like precise instruction. I took on the persona of an experienced carpenter – as anxious to show off my swagger as my skill. I placed the timber on a trestle and proceeded. I dragged the saw backways to find my start – I could see he was impressed. I pushed forward and followed the line – so far so good. Easy-peasy! Then I lost the run of myself – I tore into action, sawing like a mad man – trying to impress the Auld Man even further. I tried humming as he had done, but soon the hum turned into a grunt. The saw jammed and sprang back, I tore on. My face was getting redder and my arm was tying up. Instead of skill, I was using vigour and buck-goat rhythm. *"Woa, woa, woa, STOP!"* He had had enough. *"Let the saw do the work".*

I stopped with an indignant sigh. *"What?"* My father took his time...

"You were working fierce hard there and coming no speed. That's a great little saw – it's done a sight of cutting over the years and I sharpened it last night before I went to bed. It's the sweetest saw I think I ever had – it'd nearly go itself. All it needs is the slightest help – Let the saw do the work – just hold it nice and gentle and head it in the right direction. You'll break your wrist if you keep that up. Go again."

I didn't go any easier the next time – I didn't hear a word he said, all I was thinking was, *'Give me that saw back and I'll show you'.* My father wasn't one to lose the rag, especially when he knew he was right and a lesson needed to be learned today, it could save me some hardship and save his good saw. He went over his theory again.

"There's no point having a good edge, if you don't allow it to do its work. Giving yourself hardship is only a sign of a man who doesn't know his job. I know you're anxious to get it done, but that's where the skill comes in."

I was starting to take note, but in defiance, I picked up the saw and almost in slow motion went back at the cut. *"You mean like this!"* I said mockingly – until I realized he was right. It *was* a sweet little saw. With no aggression or fuss, it was working away goodo. No puffing or panting, just the rasp of a good edge – the smell of pine and a message understood.

In all my years as a carpenter, this was the one philosophy I clung to – *"Let the saw do the work"* – it was a metaphor for everything I did thereafter. Still – often times, exuberance got the better of me. Many a time the Auld man would say to me and Kevin – *"A good workman is easy on tools"* – that'd be after one of us had broken a handle in the pick or the axe – using our unbridled strength instead of nuance and calm.

I often studied good workmen over the years – like good sportsmen – they were never hurried – always went through a certain process – never letting the circumstance shift their protocol. I'd like to think that I was one of them – but I wasn't – not always. Too often, on a job or on a football field, when the pressure was on, I'd fret and start to saw like the bejayus. Nothing good ever came of those moments.

This day only got better – I had a few more goes on the saw – got the feel of it in my hand and liked what I felt – control. We chipped away and made progress. For the first time, I saw a project come together. We started with an empty room and now we had the frame of a press – nothing spectacular, but well made. Me and the Auld lad had tea and the nicest egg sandwiches. He told me the history of the house.

I took out that press twenty years later when I was doing it up to live there myself. I was a qualified carpenter by then. The room full of chop-saws and cordless drills and screw guns, but still the same principles applied. Let the saw do the work. As I pulled the old unit from the wall, I remembered each cut and joint, where the nail had bent and where the saw had jammed and where me and my father had tea and bread.

CHAPTER 22

Mullan Market

I n the '70's, The Troubles were belting away in Northern Ireland. We were eleven miles from the border at Ballyconnell or fifteen from Swanlinbar. British soldiers manned these borders, as did customs and excise. There were plenty who wouldn't set foot in the North – why trouble trouble? We weren't a political family – no strong views either way – we had our own troubles – trying to make ends meet at home. The North and The Troubles were in a different land as far as we were aware – we knew no one from the North and their plight and fight were theirs. We got snippets of horror over the wireless or sometimes our programmes would be interrupted on the telly – *'Would all key-holders in Limavady please return to their premises'.* But we didn't know what horror was – we treated these interruptions as exactly that – annoying and sometimes exciting bits of fall-out from another world. The horrific acts were greeted with tuts and shakes of the head, but really didn't affect our lives in any way.

My mother's side were sympathetic towards the Republican cause – their roots along the border. My mother's uncle, who was seldom mentioned, had closer involvement – but his involvement was discreet. We'd hear an odd rebel cry when there was a spree – a whiskey filled, patriotic call – but in general, we kept our heads firmly in the sand. Until there was cheap butter, that is!

Apart from The Troubles, lots of things were happening in the early seventies. In '71 – the money changed – we went decimal. One day there was 240p in the pound and the next, there was a 100. *"Is that auld money or new?"* is what went on for years. In '73, Ireland joined the European Economic Community – the EEC. There was much economic settling in to take place. Suddenly some things were much cheaper in the North. Like butter. We were devils for butter, still are. There was always bread being made and no better boys than me and my brother to eat my mother's homemade wheaten bread – with loads of butter. In the early seventies the butter was scarce and so we had started to venture up North for butter and whatever else was going cheap. We had never seen a gun in our lives – now we were being confronted by young British soldiers with loaded firearms.

Markets had sprung up around border towns. Ours was Mullan, just the far side of the border at Swanlinbar. Every Sunday the market was open for business – from

ten o'clock in the morning till around six in the evening
– it thrived. It would probably be described now, as a
farmer's market, but back then there was little in the
way of vegetables or homemade produce. We all had
those at home in plenty. No – we went to Mullan for
butter; washing powder; tools; cheap clothes and toilet
rolls. Toilet roll was a novelty – up until this, we had
always used old newspapers or moss in our outside
lavatory. We thought toilet paper was a non-essential –
a Protestant form of pampering – up there with tinned
Salmon and eating sweet-cake. But it turns out, some
had been using it for years and wearing underpants
every day and not just on Sundays and Holy days.

A Sunday with Mullan Market in it, was a great
Sunday. In the summer months, there was always
football – a match to be played or gone to – that would
always be our first calling – but once the football eased
off in the Autumn, our Sundays consisted of doing the
things, going to Mass and Mullan Market. There was
something for everyone and nothing much for anyone.

My mother browsed and thought, but never bought
anything without going back three or four times. My
father walked about and gawked and toe-poked old bits
of tools and metal, but seldom got called to bargain –
his demeanor, that of many – *'Just looking is all'*. When
I was very small, I clung on to Daddy's coat – or
waddled after Mammy as she zig-zagged over and back
between stalls and walked away empty handed. The
smell of chips always in our nostrils, but not once did
we resort to eating someone else's spuds. Our

extravagance grossly underwhelming. As we childer grew older and had managed to muster funds from somewhere – we too held tight to the shekels – a great cloud of guilt hung over our every purchase – even a music tape or coloured pen.

Sometime after me and the Auld Lad had done up the house in Druminchin, new lodgers arrived – their modest rent was invaluable, like Mammy's knitting or when Daddy worked in the Mill.

He had spent eighteen months working in McCartin's Mill in Newtowngore around '70/'71. These two young entrepreneurial brothers; Tommy and Joe McCartin had taken the local landscape by storm in the late '60's – farmers, who branched out to create a small empire of businesses, employing over three hundred people at its height. From a few acres they built – a milling operation; an engineering plant; a clothing factory; a pig farm and forestry. And they both became elected politicians. They were forward thinking, inspirational young men, whom my father really admired. In them, he saw a little bit of himself – but they were achievers – where he had walked with caution – they had dared.

The Auld Lad never could work full time as the farm and the milking took up his mornings. Then the Mill started shift work and my father took up employment. He started at five in the evening and finished at eleven – six hours at six shillings an hour and we were in clover. He did his usual work during the day, then Mammy made him a good go of egg and onion sandwiches and off he'd go. His shift was not overly exertive, whereas Mammy had to milk thirteen cows by hand and do the things on her own. Daddy got fat – Mammy got on with it. The money was welcome and then after eighteen months, the shift work was ended and we were back to square one. But there was always something – and now there was the bit of rent from Druminchin.

This particular Sunday was cloudy but dry and warm. We all set off to Mullan Market after Mass. We had a new car now – new to us – a Mark 1 Ford Escort. It's purchase had been much debated and after the cattle were sold Daddy went off all giddy one morning and brought back a shiny bluey/green two-door Escort. We thought we were great and fitted into it nice and snug – just enough room for us four in the back. Margaret was fifteen, Kevin fourteen, I was eleven and Geraldine was eight. There was no radio in the car, but my father sang - he was a good singer – the choir in the back were enthusiastic and my mother smiled.

When we got to the market, it was going through its usual sluggish, slow, pondering start. A mixture of every age and type; families from the South – enjoying their time away from the farm; young bucks from the North – looking to pimp up their cars or their bikes; young couples – using it as time together; old couples – using it as time apart. We always went our separate ways. Nobody could shop with Mammy – her persistence and tigerish haggling, were matched only by her stubbornness and patience – it was an embarrassing concoction and just too much to bear. Daddy, on the other hand, had little interest in buying anything – he was no craic. The best option was to wrangle a bit of money from either one and hang out with Margaret – she was brave enough to venture and foolish enough to buy.

The Market was our first exposure to ethnic minorities and cultural differences - we had never seen anything other than white men or women – after that they had to be either Catholic or Protestant or from Drumreilly or Aughavas. We hadn't been exposed to people with black skin or Chinese people or even Dubs. Here in Mullan, there were all sorts – brown men in turbans selling hats and haberdashery; women with nose-rings selling sheets and curtains; black men and jewellery stalls; not so black and electrical goods.

I was gawking at a stereo – a fancy tape player – it was out of my league, but one day I might be able to afford it. That was Mullan – always teasing – always tempting. Suddenly a man tapped me on my shoulder – it was Daddy, but he wasn't acting like my Auld Fella or maybe he just looked different in this environment. *"Will you come 'ere and look at this"* and he walked off. I followed him – he went to a tool stall. His rapport with the bearded man who's stall it was, was that of a pair who had spent a considerable amount of time together. My father picked up a Tennon Saw and handed it to me – this was a more precise tool than his sweet old hand saw – we had them at school – I had explained it to him, the day we were at the house in Druminchin. *"Is that a good saw?"*, he asked – there was an air of excitement in his voice – and pride – here he had a son heading for six foot – a lad good with his hands. At the time I didn't understand the moment or feel it or know that it was so rare and so wonderful – but I didn't let him down. I took the saw in my hand, felt it's weight and balanced it, I turned it and studied it and with careful consideration in my voice, I said, *"Yea... feels like a good saw to me"*. My father turned to the bearded man – handed him a pound and some change and said, *"Ya see, I told you this lad would know"*.

As the stall owner took the saw in for wrapping – a few big drops came down on the market and then a dirty shower of rain. Me and Daddy stood in under the canopy of the stall, out of the drip. *"Where are ye from, men?"* your man asked us in his strong Northern accent. *"Leitrim"*, we replied. *"Ah Lovely Leitrim – we get a lot from Leitrim up here – nice people – Leitrim people"*. That's when me and my father realised that this fella was full of auld sweet talk and not worth staying dry for. We got our new saw back in a flimsy plastic bag and we headed for the car. Most were caught in the rain like us and some were even buying umbrellas and cheap rain-coats. We had coats at home and the rain falls lighter on those who have coats at home. When we got to the car, the others were huddled around – drenched. We all slid in together and headed for home. I had to sit on the new saw in case we got stopped by customs. Mammy had a thorny plant up her dress and Daddy couldn't see out with steam.

CHAPTER 23

The Silver Coin

As the '70's wore on – we began to leave the old ways behind. I still wet the bed, but had the widest pair of bell-bottoms, if not the longest, for going to Mass. We still didn't have a bathroom – but we had a decent car, a tractor, a washing machine, a television and three out of four children at big school. Apart from sporting ambition, I had little else in my head. School was to be endured until I found my calling – truck driving; welding; anything other than farming. I could see how any injection of cash affected our lives – in a good way – I couldn't wait to get my hands on some of that.

Everyone at school had BBC and UTV television – of course they had – we were always the last to get everything – even when there was a bad flu going, we were the last to get it. Everyone else taking days off school – probably getting pampered by their mothers and us still standing at the cross, waiting for the bus with sleeves of green snot and not a bit remarks passed on our minor sniffles or our hasky coughs. *"You're all right"*, my mother would say, *"it'd take more than that to keep you away, if it was a football match"*. Of course, she was right. Still, an odd day off would have been nice, like when I got the measles. I had been unwell for a week and no one believed me, then I got these itchy lumps and I was kept at home – now that I had proof of my illness. It was heaven. Sups of tea in bed and egg in a cup. Being tucked in and getting sympathy was something very alien to our way of living. It was a good day you were sick. Everything tasted better with the bit of love in it, or was that just butter? Maybe love and butter are the same thing – you wouldn't give butter to someone you didn't like – no – that's when you'd take out the margarine.

We had been at Daddy this long time about getting more stations on the telly. It turns out that the signal for the English stations was coming from Enniskillen and our house was on the wrong side of the hill – of course it was. We'd need to put our aerial up so high above the house, that it would necessitate a stay or two. Everyone else had their aerial on their chimney – but our chimney wasn't stable enough for a high aerial – of course it wasn't! Eventually, in a moment of weakness, the Auld Man went with a plan to hoist an aerial up on a wooden pole made from a tall conifer which had been cut down especially for the job. It was an afternoon of great tension – the guilt surrounding this erratic notion was palpable, and all our efforts that day were aimed at keeping Daddy humoured – saying the right thing –

encouraging him, without patronizing – he was in a volatile state – knowing that this chore was, at best, an extravagant use of time – or at worst – a total waste of time. The other thing was – he hadn't a clue what he was doing. He grumbled and exaggerated his anguish with 'tut's and 'but's and 'now look at this's – he was a man searching for failure, when it was just around the corner. The pole was hoisted with an aerial attached, it was turned and twisted until the faintest of figures came into our kitchen via the telly – *"There's something there"*, we shouted and there was – something – the slightest turn of the pole might bring them to life – what could it be?

"What can you see?"

"It looks like people walking about"

"Do they look English?"

"Turn it a bit more – Woahhh"

"Well, what do you see now?"

"They're swimming – it's swimming – they're racing"

"Well that's not Irish – we'll tighten it up so"

"It's not a great picture"

"I'd say it's as good as we'll get"

And it was – our ability to accept blur and fuzz was second to none. Once again in my short life – the expectation way outweighed the reality. Now we had the other stations – the BBC and UTV – English ones swimming, that we could barely see. The tallish pole stood at the side of the scullery for years. It looked unstable and it was – bull-wire was used to stay it. A whole lot of effort for little reward. We could hardly watch the telly that night with disappointment – not so much that the picture was fuzzy – but some strange melancholy fell over the six of us – a realisation that no joy would fly in from the sky – not the northern sky or any sky – not into our house. We were stuck with RTE.

On a Thursday night, a few neighbours had been in playing cards – McCaffery and Hugh Murray. As they were getting ready to leave, Hugh Murray asked me, would I help him fill a few barrels of water at Clogher river on Saturday morning. *"I'll pay you"*, he said somewhere in the conversation. He had said lots of things – he talked about the recent dry spell; the last dry spell; other even less notable dry spells – McCaffery was getting thirsty with all the talk of drought, but all I was thinking of was the other thing he said. *"I'll pay you"*. I had never got paid before for anything other than my first holy Communion and Confirmation. I was already saving up – I didn't know how much he was going to give me or how long this dry spell would last, but I was saving up for Lego – or maybe not Lego, I was getting big for Lego – maybe, it was time to start saving up for a lorry. I couldn't sleep for the next two nights thinking of money – working out the sums – adding up and multiplying. I was fairly sure that I'd be fit for the work – what was the work again? – Oh aye – filling barrels of water. No problem.

On Saturday morning, I was ready – it was eight o'clock. I was unable to help do the things, because I was going to work. *"Hugh Murray won't stir till at least ten"*, I was told – still, better to be ready and not using up my energy on unpaid work, I thought. My stance was not tolerated, but it was worth a try. I did my bit that morning – slowly and with an ear cocked for Hugh – but he didn't come – he didn't save me from the drudge at home. We finished the things and had the breakfast – my second breakfast. It was Saturday – a little more relaxed without school and lunches and homework not done. The Auld Man picked up the paper. Mammy sewed something on to something else – silence. Silence was a rare thing in our house – I'm sure it was in any house where childer are small. The silence in my life has always been filled with expectation of things to come, or the disappointment of what has gone. This morning, it was one turning into the other.

Then, between the rustle of the paper and the sigh of a stitching Mother, I heard hooves and the iron shoeing of a cart on the Toome road. Hugh Murray was on the move. His horse and cart were one of the last around. I could just about remember ours – I had got the tail-end of that time and way – slow, ponderous and glorious in equal measure. This tired morning in late autumn was interrupted with distant clattering and my expectation was, for once, coming to fruition. I calmly rose from my sitting and said, *"That's Hugh – I better go"*. My father looked over the paper. Not his normal glance – he looked at me – all of me – from my footwear to my thought filled head. He said, *"Aye, you better"*. My mother smiled to herself, marking the moment, but not disturbing it. I went to the gate to wait.

Beyond the piers of our gate, there's an embankment which separates our old garden from the road – a place where moss and ivy and wild strawberries grow – a place we sat to wait. In the coming years, I would sit here often, waiting for lifts and rendezvous'; for Tom Mimna's Volkswagen Beetle; for Patsy Wrynn's crockety bus. Today I was waiting to go to my first mornings work – my first wage – a silver coin was my hope – please don't let it be copper.

The sound of Hugh's brigade was as far away as ever – Hugh Murray was never a man to hurry the world around him – cautious as he was fair – whatever time he took, he took it with care and used it without assumption. The noise eventually got louder as he came to McCaffery's turn and then I caught site of the old chestnut mare – head down and dawdling, Hugh sat behind in the well-kept lead painted cart. Beside him, two wooden water barrels, two buckets, two apples – one for me, one for the horse.

"You're a great man", he said as he pulled up. 'Nelly' – the mare stood, eyes down. The cart was higher than I remembered. I put my foot on the spoke of the wheel and I climbed on board. There was something evocative about our jaunt to the cross – the last of the horsemen go sauntering by. Every day was a Saturday to Nelly. She got us there eventually – a carriage of slow-moving parts and men. At the cross I hopped off and opened the gap into our meadow and Nelly pulled up alongside the river. Without instruction, I whipped off my shoes and socks and stepped in. Hugh handed me a bucket; I filled

it and handed it to him; he took it and handed me the empty one. We filled one barrel and then me and Nelly had our apples. I quickly returned to my station and we filled another one. That was it, that was the job – it wasn't rocket science – it wasn't much, but progress was made that day and I liked the feel of industry – such as it was. Hugh handed me a towel to dry my feet and I did – I put back on my socks and shoes and when the load was headed for home, I closed the gap. I sat with the man who gave me my first start – 10p – 5p a barrel – a silver coin and the water splashed and churned. I liked the feeling of going home with more than I had come out with. Hugh Murray was decent a man.

CHAPTER 24

Harmonica

Coming up to Christmas '76 – I was taking stock. Why was Santy not more celebrated during the year? Surely a man of such generosity and kindness, should be a bigger part of our everyday lives. There were ones at school who would laugh at that notion – especially the ones wearing the heavy-metal jackets. Santy wasn't on their Christmas card list – why not? Was I missing something?

I would soon be twelve, I had grown to almost six foot – I had won an under 14 County title for playing football, I had a drawer full of medals for running, jumping, throwing, buck lepping, long pucking and a bonny-baby contest, that I just missed out on. I had survived a bog-hole, but won turf, caught turf, wheeled turf, tossed turf and drank tea from a bottle in the bog – I drank tea in the meadow too and often when spreading dung. I had mowed hay, raked, tedded and turned it – I made cocks, laps and hand-shakes – headed, drew, pitched, took in and when there was no place for any more hay in the shed, I tramped and packed it. I had ploughed, guggered, shoveled, dug and eaten more spuds than was good for me and I could milk and let out the cows and still Santy and Jesus were my only friends – the only ones I could trust.

In a wrestling match after a 'Poineer' meeting, John Prior had caught me by the balls and squeezed till my eyes nearly popped out – what was that about? It was the first time I became aware of my privates. On my first school tour at the Tech, we were after being to the Zoo and as I was getting back on our fancy coach – one of the 'Secretarial Girls' bent over with a low top and I got a buzzin' in me bell-bottoms – that hadn't happened before – I had to sit down. I thought a reptile had escaped from the Zoo and crept into me trousers. Worse than that – he had made himself a nest and was forever sticking his head up at the most inopportune moments. I had sinus related headaches, growing pains and an eating disorder and yet there was still hope – because one day I might play for Leitrim.

But for the moment it was winter and all that was on my mind, was Christmas. I was too big for toys, so I might as well make a start on my musical career. I announced I was asking for a harmonica that year. We never actually wrote to Santy – he didn't need that sort of communication – his magic is stronger than that. You just have to wish – wish out loud when someone's in the room – a few times – and then at breakfast.

Christmas didn't take up much time in our house, apart from in some of our heads. There was a few nights when Mammy took out a box of Christmas cards and an address book – she wrote, addressed and sealed with the same determination as when she was knitting or milking cows – it was a job that had to be done and now it was. A few cards and envelopes would be put one side for the Auld Lad to fill in – cards to his brothers, sisters and mother – it was a chore that he hated, yet when it came to it, he would sit and ponder what to write, careful with words and not just a matter of getting it done. He was of the generation who had been put from writing left-handed, by means of a ruler across the knuckles. He wasn't scarred physically or mentally by this, just a bit bemused was all. He'd say, *"That's the way it was them times"*. He liked school – prided himself in his spelling and arithmetic – yet admitted he wasn't the best in his house at it. His older brother, Michael was a whiz-kid at the sums and the spelling and his younger brother, Kevin, was a priest.

As Christmas approached – so did the familiar sound of the postman's Honda 50. John Donnelly was our postman – a low to the ground, larger than life, ball of energy. He was a well-known figure in the locality and beyond. He was a star actor with the Carrigallen Community Players – he always had the funny lines or maybe it was his natural timing and ability that made them funny. *"There's ones in there, who'd make pure shite of a good line"*, is what he'd say about his fellow drama folk – not the most generous of actors on stage, but never turned down the generosity of others while doing the post. This postman always came in. He had tea in most houses, dinner in some, bottles of beer were welcome, but whiskey was his king. John loved whiskey and most loved to give it to him – in return, you'd get – a few letters, yes – but more than that, you'd get the best of good yarns, guffaws of laughter and a morning pleasantly interrupted by joy and misbehaviour. We loved to see John coming. I'd be listening out from early morning – then you'd hear the bubble-bubble of his bike coming at Gorthaheeran. He often stopped at our house with no letters. He'd get off his bike and we'd hear the clip-clop of his wooden clogs which he had specially made – so that people would know when to get out the whiskey.

He was a tonic! He and my father, along with several others, had re-formed the under-age football club in Carrigallen. There was always football to be talked – he'd tell you you were good, if you brought him more whiskey – and if you kept it to him, you'd be an all-star by dinnertime. He often stayed to dine – said our spuds were better than most. He was a fine gardener himself. He took a few ridges with us for a year or two – helped us shovel and spray and dig. He was our postman; our friend; our coach and our clown and when Christmas came, he brought Bringing Christmas Cheer to a new level.

Because of John's fondness of whiskey, poteen and punch – people stocked up in December and everywhere he went, he was offered a taste. He didn't like to refuse – with the result, he would be flutered as he headed back the road for Carrigallen. Several times, he came off his bike and broke... wind. He had also broken his leg a few times and so a lesson learned. These last few years, he'd bring a driver. He'd leave the bike at home and get one of his many pals from about the town to drive him around, delivering post, devouring feeds and drinking good health and Happy Christmas to one and all. Of course, the driver couldn't be left out, so he ended up drunk as a skunk too. *"What are you getting for Christmas, big man?"* asked the postman. I was tentative with my reply.

"A harmonica"

"A Monica who?"

"No, a harmonica – a French fiddle – that you play"

"You could play with a Monica, if you got the right one – Are you not a bit big for Santy?"

"I'm still only eleven"

"Ah shite, you're nearly as big as your father"

The postman meant no harm, but it put me back a tad – I started thinking about the whole Santy thing. What if the rumours were true – what if Santy has a cut-off point and what if I had reached it? I broached the subject with my mother – she said it was alright to ask for stuff right up until I was thirteen – I intended to be driving a lorry for McCartin's by the time I was thirteen – I couldn't be riding two horses and the size of me. Childhood was starting to get messy.

A week before Christmas, the Auld Pair were away – they had gone to buy a heater for the parlour that no one went into. I got curious and I started to search. I wasn't sure what I was looking for, but for the first time in my life, I felt there were secrets being kept – somewhere. I searched and found all Daddy's treasure – on top of things. I went to the spare room where Granny once slept and where my grandfather had been laid out. On top of the wardrobe, I found a small shiny box and inside it something that played music. An instrument for a cowboy on the lonesome trail, just in case Santy doesn't turn up.

I was left shocked and disappointed. Is this the way my life will unfold. What is real and what is really important? I put on my football boots and grabbed the ball – I went to the field in front of the house – I hadn't been there in months. Although it was December, the field was holding up well – not as wet as I expected. I simply kicked the ball into the sky and caught it – I felt the leather in my hands – this was real. I stayed there till it was nearly dark and the Auld Pair came home. My world was getting sorted out – kick by kick. I could always rely on football – it would never let me down. How wrong was that notion?

On Christmas morning, we all woke early – Geraldine was very excited to see what Santy brought. I kept a close eye on my older sister and brother – what did their eyes say when I looked up close? They looked at me inquisitively – knowing something was up – knowing exactly what was up. We went downstairs to the parlour – that's where the Christmas tree was and where we had asked Santy to leave the presents this year. Before this, he left them at the end of the bed – this year would be more like Christmas on the telly. A pop-up Christmas tree with lights and tinsel and Mammy had told us to put on the new gas heater a while. That took a while – turn on the gas – hold down the ignition button half way for fifteen seconds and then give her the holly – that was the theory. Christmas was nearly over by the time it was lit.

Then Geraldine went first – a doll and clothes. And then it was my turn – it looked small, but heavy enough. I opened it up and there it was – a harmonica. It was a bit like the one on top of the wardrobe – but wasn't. I don't think it was. Thank God for Santy!

None of my family play an instrument – Granny quenched that line a long time ago. I often wondered if my grandfather on Daddy's side was musical or if he just played a musical instrument. There is a difference. The chances are, it's just not in our blood. Maybe Granny was right to wean him off the fiddle – maybe he was giving her a headache. The Auld Fella said I was playing the harmonica wrong, when I had a go on that Christmas morning. I looked to others for encouragement, but it wasn't forthcoming. The fact that I couldn't play the harmonica well on my first attempt satisfied everyone, including me – that I just wasn't born to be a cowboy.

CHAPTER 25

More Granny

We only had the Escort a short while and it was already a tight squeeze to get everyone in – especially when we weren't wet. We avoided all going in the car at the one time, where possible, but sometimes we just had to scrunch up. This was one of those times. We were heading off to Manorhamilton to see our aunt Peggy and Granny. It was January and this was our Christmas visit – there might be presents waiting for us down there. We were sure there would be presents, because Granny was good and aunt Peggy was the best.

Margaret brought the tape recorder and her new tape of ABBA. It was alien, having the sound of real music in the car. I tried to imagine us being a cool family and having a cool car, with it's own stereo. But that image was too hard to muster. We looked like a crowd of 'thicks' with a tape player in the back, fighting over which song we'd play – fast forward – rewind – if truth be told, I preferred that sound – the busy winding mechanics of the machine – absolutely baffling or at least intriguing – or maybe it's because I wasn't really an ABBA fan.

We knew all the landmarks on the way to Manor – even with our eyes closed – in the dark on the way home – we knew where we were. We had done this journey once a month since Granny moved out of our house and into Boley Hill. It was seven years and if we were getting big and hard to fit in the car, she was getting older and milder and further away. She had discovered Bingo in Manorhamilton – four or five times a week by all accounts. A replacement feed of stimulation when your services elsewhere are no longer required. She lived just around the corner from her daughter. Peggy's gang were real townies – only a minute from the shop and preferred soccer to Gaelic. But Peggy's husband, Bernie, had land outside the town, so they weren't completely soft. Aunt Peggy, Bernie and our three cousins – Mairéad, Eugene and Kevin were a perfect detox when life on the farm became too much. It was a change of scenery and although the space was cramped, they had a good telly and you'd get great tea with lots of bought ham and foosie. We always went to Peggy's first and after eating our fill, we'd call into Granny.

Granny's house was tiny, but welcoming – she had the tiniest of lawns at the front, which we often mowed – she took particular umbrage to buttercups growing in it. Her sitting room was cosy and because of the day and time of day that we'd be there – 'The Sunday Matinee' was always left on in the background in case the conversation got scarce. Sometimes on these visits, one of my uncles would be home or my aunts from America – and Granny's mood would fluctuate on a par with where they stood in the pecking order.

My Uncle Father Kevin was a missionary priest – spent most of his time in Kenya and then Sudan – *"just out with the black fellas"*, he'd say – keeping his work on a 'by the way' footing for our sake. He felt we had little interest in his efforts, as we seldom asked – (we never asked) as he seemed reluctant to expand. Truth be told, he was risking life and limb to be out there. He provided practical and spiritual assistance to a very volatile people – we thought there was no one had it as tough as we had. He dealt with them and us by way of patience and a great sense of humour and calm. A most caring man. Granny was fierce proud of him, as we were, we just didn't like to say.

My Uncle Michael was a force of nature – he had get-up-and-go, and he did – all the time. He was quick and smart and wrestled life till someone let out a squeal – a buzzing, stinging bee that would never let you lie down or back away and could always find the positive, regardless of where it hid. We were lucky to have such diverse relations. My aunt Monica was elegant and pronounced and Aunt Theresa was a scoundrel – a poet – a blundering, bubbling basket case of love and compassion – not an ounce of wit or wickedness – born-again and again and again until she held Jesus so tight, he had to say, *"That's enough now, Theresa, you come along with me".* My aunt Theresa always felt especially akin to me – and I kind of hid from her. She was a wonderful woman, but I was wary – even afraid. I could see she had magic and passion and oceans of personality, but she also had vulnerability about her and so close to the surface. Maybe I was scared it was contagious. I couldn't live that close to the edge. All my emotions would have to be carefully locked in and the keys hung in the right order – I wouldn't mind dipping into them every now and then – but I could not be like my aunt Theresa, wearing my blood and guts on my sleeve.

I had another aunt – Aunt Vera. She was in America from when she was very young and never came home. I never met her and my father only saw her a couple of times in fifty years.

We sat in Granny's house in silence; she said to turn up the telly. Bing Crosby was singing – who could resist Bing Crosby playing a priest in 'The Bells of St Mary's'. His soothing voice sent Daddy off to sleep – Mammy's instinct was to make tea, but it wasn't her house. The four of us young ones would take tea anytime especially if there was foosie. Daddy didn't snore like Granny – but his absence from the conversation was awkward. Mammy and Granny didn't really have that much to say to each other. You can only ask about the bingo so often – after that – there's no winners. Suddenly Granny said, *"I suppose Peggy gave you some lunch earlier".* We all smirked to one another at the posh way she said 'lunch' – no one ever called it lunch up our way – it's just because Granny had spent some time in America and now Manorhamilton and mostly because she was showing off with her lawn and her full panel at bingo in Glenfarne on the Thursday night before. *"Sure, we might have a wee drop to waken us up before we head off"* – unlike Mammy to say that. Granny scolded as she was right comfortable sitting watching Bing.

The routine for tea in Granny's was simple – be ready to help, but don't get in her way. The wee back kitchen was fierce small and the few times Mammy went in there with Granny, she nearly didn't come back out. Although Granny had shrunk of late, she was still a fair width and she was very conscious of this. The times Mammy had gone into the kitchen after her – they had got jammed between the sink and the wall and neither one would retreat. We called it 'The Battle of Boley Hill'. There was nothing said and there would have been nothing but politeness between them– but there was still a leftover feud. Sometimes Granny would try to give Mammy money – just to get something for us. The hackles would be up right away and pride upset. They would clasp hands – the money somewhere amid their fingers – and a flailing arm wrestle would take place – Granny ready to guzzle her daughter-in-law – Mammy holding back from throttling her. And then my mother would take the money, but at least she had made her point.

This afternoon was different. We let Granny into the kitchen on her own and bit by bit, she handed out the things for the tea. There was no fuss, but it took a while.

We were getting hungry. This wasn't meant to be a meat tea as we had already eaten – but she handed out a horrid go of cake and biscuits – we were licking our lips. Mammy started to do this winking thing that she does – when decorum is required. The winking suggested that we not go to town on the cake and sweet stuff, as it would be bad for us or give us some sort of satisfaction that we didn't deserve. We answered her wink with an opposite, opening and widening of the eyes and raising of our eyebrows. Granny, who was oblivious to our not so subtle sign language, finally handed out the teapot and jug and it was time to wake Daddy and tuck in – or not.

Everything was piled onto a small table – everyone got a dainty cup and the tea was poured. There was lots of, *"This is lovely..."* *"Ah God, this is great..."* *"Ya wouldn't get this in a hotel..."* *"That's lovely tea".* Granny said it was only a cup of tea and a biscuit – that she had ham but – but she obviously didn't want to give it to us. A ham sandwich would have been nice, but no matter. Again, there was a general glance towards Mammy, to see if we could go for a bit of cake. Her eyes said, alright, but go easy. We all went for the biggest bit and our daintiness got muddled with our greed and some finger fighting ensued at the lower end of the table. Not to worry as Mammy was keeping a close eye.

There was more, *"That's lovely cake..."* *"Where did you get that cake..."* *"I think that might be the nicest cake I've ever eaten",* with Granny saying, *"Eat it up there, it'll only go to loss".* My uninformed opinion at the time, was that the cake wouldn't go to loss, as Granny looked like a woman who ate a lot of cake or a lot of ham or a lot of something, but of course, I didn't say that and with the most recent invitation still warm, we all dived in again – without any eye-negotiation with Mother. Margaret in particular, looked like she was enjoying herself and after her second slice, she had a third and then ignoring Mammy's daggered looks – she clinked the fourth and Mammy with her subtleness stashed away at this stage, reached under the table and with her pincer like grip, gave my poor sister an unmerciful nip. Margaret's face was suddenly showing surprise, terror, embarrassment and pain, all at one and the same time. Her eyes welled up and, big and all as she was, she screamed at the top of her voice and burst out crying. Granny was alarmed – *"Good heavens, ya poor child, what is it?"* – My sister couldn't hold it in – she looked at her mother and said, *"My Mammy nipped me"*.

CHAPTER 26

Number 4

At last I was twelve – at last I had caught up with some of the others in my class at school. There were thirty-six of us in first year at the Tech. Up until now, I was the only one who was eleven – most were thirteen, but some were twelve and so for a while, I'd fit in. Our class was split in two – X and Y. Mr. Creed came in the third day and said they were going to split the class – he said, *"Give me eighteen names"*, and so the most forward, or the most auld fashioned ones, gave their names first and so, first year X were a class of wasters and show-offs and Y was for the shy and studious. I was in X.

If the list had been made the first day, I would have been in Y. Because I was shy too and quiet or reserved – whatever way you want to describe a piddling, petrified pupil, who wasn't even old enough to have pimples, let alone an opinion. I had no standing whatsoever. When I got on the Monkey-Bus that first morning, I was a nobody. By the time I got through the bare-knuckle initiation with Oliver Reilly – I had really swollen hands... but I had earned some respect – yes, for being a fierce thick young fella, but respect all the same. Within the next hour, I was sliding down an embankment behind Room No 2 and through a well-manicured hedge. Some of the Killashandra ones thought it might be good craic to slide down the steep hill on that nice soft morning in September and it was and I joined in because, now, everyone was doing it. The school grounds-man and caretaker, Jimmy Higgins was not so impressed. A gruff man at best – he entered the frame, just as I was creating a world record for 'The Long Slide & Hedge Toss'. He had his eye on me from then on.

At lunch break, I headed straight for the football pitch on the hill at the back of the school – if you could call it a pitch. It ran at right angles to the steep slope. Two sets of goalposts about a hundred yards apart. The side-line at the top of the hill lined with whins and the lower side, lined with egg-bushes. Regardless of which way you were playing, you always had one foot on higher ground. It was a narrow pitch too, so very often the ball and most of the players ended up in the egg-bushes. Frustrations always ran high in the Tech field. If the ball cleared the egg-bushes, it could run for two hundred yards down the hill to the back of the pre-fabs at the back of the school.

On this lunch break, my first ever lunch break at the Tech – there were 4th year's having a game up on the slanty pitch. Football was one place I wasn't shy and when I asked to join in, I was told to fuck off. This language was new to me – we never cursed at home – not without replacing the first letter at least. When tempers got really frayed at home – we might hear words like 'Bucking' or 'Rolix', but now because I was at an institute of further learning, the curses were spelled properly. I was being told in no uncertain terms, to fuck off and I didn't like it.

Martin Reilly – a typical 4th year at the time – denim from top to toe... including his teeth – was standing daring me to make a move for the ball – I did and he didn't like it – I was suddenly surrounded by denim and danger. They were looking for a fight, I didn't know enough to walk away.

I was never in a proper fight – Kevin gave me a bit of a timbering when I was younger and we often wrestled at school – I even had my balls squeezed by John Prior, but nothing as potentially dangerous as this. Strangely I wasn't too perturbed – I knew I could take pain – I had the swollen paws to prove it and I had taken some fair wallops from teachers in the past and my mother when our stars didn't align. How bad could it be? These weren't that tough – I could see beyond the denim. In my subconscious, I came up with a strategy – get to the higher ground and swing like billyo – and I did. I had forgotten that I was so big and they were mostly townies. I'm not saying I beat them up – but I had stood my ground and by the time the bell rang, I had gained more respect – albeit, once again for being a shocking thick young fella.

I headed back down to the school with my inflated hands and ego, only to be met by Mick Duignan and Jimmy Higgins. At their core, these two men were very alike – Duignan was, first and foremost, a man of nature and of the people, who's responsibility it was, to harness nature – he taught Science and Biology, but it was his philosophy that was at the heart of the school. Give the young men and women of the region a little scientific and technical knowhow to go along with their graft and toil and you'll get young farmers, who have a confidence and trust in science to help maximize the land's potential. Encourage rural based trades and professions... he was a man before his time. But that didn't mean we all had to be 'thicks'! – numb-skulls as he called us. And here was me, coming back down the hill of illusion – bruised and battered and quickly becoming a numb-skull of gigantic proportions.

Jimmy Higgins was a local – no degrees or diplomas to hold him back, just good honest to God adherence to nature and to nature's way. He planted and sowed in the school garden and greenhouse, just as he did at home. He took advice from the headmaster when he cared to – he threw it back to him, when he was done. These two men communicated in chewed up grunts and nasal harmonics – opinions and hairy-ned eyebrows in tandem as they glanced in my direction.

"And here's young Rourke, like a mad bullock jumping through a hedge – what kind of a ninny-hammer do we have here? Another Drumeela lampoon no doubt – as much brains as you'd put in a

worm. You're lucky we caught you in time 'a Mhac' – we don't want you going to seed, before your first lunchbreak is out. Your sister and brother haven't set the world alight, but at least they're quiet and easy on fuel. You're mad to be important and horsing everyone out of your way – like it's an exercise in brute strength – which it's not. We have a place for the likes of you, if this sort of behaviour persists – Room Number 4 is our detention centre – a place of radical reform and writing out lines – you don't want to go there, but you will, if you don't change your stride. I'm hoping you're just a rabbit caught in the headlights – so for now a kindly warning – the next time, I'll knock your block off, ya big, thick, overgrown nincompoop".

Jimmy added some guttural aside and that was it. My first telling off. I put my head down and walked on – that was a great telling off – this man had style and some great words – I'd look them up, but I doubt they'd even exist. I was a little disappointed that I had missed out on Number 4, but the day was still young. I had changed since this morning. I had come a long way from when I was having my porridge and the little excited head on me. In the space of a few hours, I had knuckles scrunched, a hedge flattened and my first fight completed – I had stumbled my way into the bad books of the principle without really opening my mouth. I was on a stroll down bad-boy avenue.

I continued my walk over by the pre-fabs and past Jimmy Higgins' well-kept garden and glass house. I could see John McGerty and another first year coming around at No 6 – you'd know by the gimp of them, that their day had been a lot tamer than mine. I called out – just as I did, I spotted a row of pulled turnips on the garden ridge – I was dying for a kick of a ball, but a turnip would do. I unleashed a powerful shot towards the greenhouse – never thinking that my shooting would be so spot on, but it was. The shattering glass took away from the anguish on my face after kicking such a deadweight missile. The next thing I heard, was my name being shouted, followed by an accurate description.

"Rourke – ya pup – ya brat – you're nothing but a tramp – you'll pay for that, ya good-for-nothing frigger – you'll be in number 4 till ya have a beard, ya big long string of misery".

I was okay with that – I needed number 4 to bookend my day. Jimmy Higgins marched me down to the main school. In the girls door as we called it, by the girls toilets and the 'Home Economics Room' and up the corridor to the staff room. Opposite the staffroom, was the famous No 4 – the detention centre and Science room – beside that was the woodwork room and the boys toilets and then there was a big wide stairway to the metalwork room and No 2 and that was all of the main building – there were two sets of pre-fabricated structures which held five more general classrooms and that was it. Modest and disciplined – as I was about to find out.

Jimmy Higgins told me to wait in the corridor while he played 'clash-bag' and went off telling on me. He came back out of the office with a smirk of satisfaction – I wasn't sure if it was because of my impending punishment or because he felt like a teacher coming out of the staffroom. He purred off with himself and I waited.

Eamon Daly appeared. He was the vice principle – a hippy – shoulder length hair and beard – how long had he spent in No 4? He was in his early thirties and calmness personified – I didn't know whether he was going to punish me or baptize me.

"Damn it all, Seamus – I thought you'd be a model student; a fine footballer; an ambassador for your family and Drumeela, you really are the last person I expected to see standing here. You'll have to aim higher than Number 4".

Mr. Daly had his own way of tugging back a galloping mule – no intimidation or histrionics – just empathy and kindness and reasonable consideration. What a concoction to be throwing at a young fella on his first day.

CHAPTER 27

Time

I Knelt beside the bed. It was time for prayer and reflection. This sounds like a wholesome and routinely Catholic act of discipline and worship. It was and it wasn't. It was mainly habit. I'd say most Irish kids did it at the time – it was part of our upbringing. Wash your hands – comb your hair – say your prayers – go to bed. I wasn't as good at praying as my brother and I'd say mine was a whole lot more selfish.

"Please God, make me taller, thinner, faster and a better footballer – don't mind my family and keeping them safe – they're safe enough – it's me you need to concentrate on – I have special needs. I really want to be a superstar and if you grant me that, I think I could do some real good."

Then, I'd get into bed all smug – thinking I knew more than God. Sometimes I got back out of bed and went at him again:

"Dear God, if you really wanted me to spend my life standing in gaps – why didn't you make my arms out

of 'Wavin' pipe. You know, you set me aside for
something great, try and remember what it was and
don't just throw be back in with the normal, decent,
caring ones. That's no craic! I want more Lego and
nicer lunches – Thank you and sorry about Easter"

The truth is, we did talk to God – all the time – It's just, some of us used him as a sort of wishing well. We were lucky in our family, we never had tragedy or trauma to deal with – we were just your ordinary rural Irish family of the time – we were healthy – well fed and strong as jinnets – but some of us weren't that fond of the drudgery. Some of us wanted more! And not more of the same – something else. Something to break up the monotony.

I was getting to a stage in my physical development, where I wanted challenges. Kevin was streets ahead of me in terms of physical strength – but I was catching up. Back then, we'd ask for no better craic, than to have a meadow of hay ready for cocking and to see a dark cloud hovering. We'd turn the work at hand into a game – how quick can we stack this meadow? How fast can we spread this dung? From as young as ten, our bodies were starting to respond to the tasks we set before them. In winter, when there was foddering to be done, we'd load ourselves with hay, and race up the hills. In summer, it was turf or the spuds or the never-ending cycle of mowing, turning, tedding hay and then you weren't even half way. The Auld Pair might have gotten rid of the horses in the late sixties – well now they had two donkeys and although we were hard fed and one still wetting the bed –we made light of any day's labour.

At that time, my father began to see the farm through different eyes. Projects that up till now, seemed too daunting – all of a sudden, looked doable. He now had help. There was also the added incentive of a government grant at the time. It was for land drainage and reclamation and our father applied. Most of Mammy's homeplace in Druminchin was taken over by whins (gorse) – dozens of tiny fields almost meeting in the middle with whins and the rest was rushes. The Leitrim terrain, like that of West Cavan and North Longford is made up of drumlin hills. Shallow soil and dauby clay don't make ideal farm land, but there are patches of promise and fertility – which only lead to our farmers' biggest curse – hope. There are good farms in this region, but they're unlikely to have O's or Mc's attached to the family name – a legacy from our recent past and British occupation – *'To Hell or to Connacht'*, I think someone once said – well if there was a hell *in* Connacht – it must have been in our fields and it's fires... when we were burning whins.

In 1977, '78 and '79, our attempts to get rid of the creeping gorse were futile. Whins grow back – they need to be stubbed. We could have contracted men with diggers and bull-dozers – but these were expensive and not nearly enough hardship. My father had a better plan – now that he had help. *"We'll get a 'stubber' for the tractor"* – a bit of a thing like a hook that he put on the back of a Massy Ferguson 165 and then took in to shout and roar. He'd curse too – always replacing the first letter of course. *"Stand harder on the bucking thing"*. He'd ask us to stand on the back of this yoke, so it got a grip and then when it got a grip – when it actually grabbed the afore mentioned whin by the roots and attempted to pull – the front of the tractor would rise up in the air like a stallion, and so we'd have to go from standing on the back to sitting on the front of the tractor. Our health and safety badges firmly shoved up our backsides at this stage. We weren't creating farmable land, by the way – we were just creating space for the rushes to grow. Every evening when we got home from school and on Saturday, if there wasn't hay or turf, we'd be stubbing whins. These journeys to the 'Congo' of our farm were not appreciated back then and certainly don't deserve any more than a page of a book.

You hear of men being at one with nature – my father and brother, for the most part, were in a brawl with nature. Their obsession with land was like my obsession with football – we both fought the good fight, but ultimately, we both got spat out. But, at least now, the whins only grow in the hedges – their coconut perfumed yellow blossoms are such a part of these rolling drumlin hills in the springtime. I think when I'm away, it's them I miss most of all. I fought them on the frontline – they retreated as did I. Maybe we have a mutual respect for each other – when I die – I hope I die in spring with the blossoms still on the whins.

One spring, around Easter time, there was an awful calamity in our house – the clock stopped. It was an electric clock and couldn't be fixed till after the holidays. There were other clocks in the house, but we kept looking at the stopped one, because it was the good clock.

Time was a confusing commodity in our house at the best of times. Sometimes, we didn't go by it. For example, in October, when the clocks went back, we'd leave them as they were for a few weeks, till we'd get the spuds dug. This meant an extra hour in the evening when we'd get home from school, for digging. The Auld Fella called this 'taking back time'. To add to the confusion, he referred to the time we went by during the summer, as 'New Time' and then the winter time would be, 'Auld Time'. This was fine – but sometimes, we'd change some clocks and not others and then when Daddy asked, *"Is that Auld Time or New Time?"* We'd say New Time, because it was new to us – but really it was Auld Time. The time changing in spring was always welcome, because it was giving us an extra hour in the evening and it was also called, 'New Time' – so, all the clocks were changed right away – no point in taking back time that's not there – but then the good clock stopped that Easter, just after the time had changed.

Because of these two monumental happenings, we were left with a clock in the parlour telling Auld Time – a carriage clock telling New Time and the good clock that was stopped – telling us, it was a quarter to three. Time for the 'Passion' in Drumeela!

When we got to Drumeela – there was nobody there. We were three-quarters of an hour early. Mammy was raging. We decided to go in to the chapel or there'd be a row in the car. I sat in on my own – about five rows from the back – on the men's side. I was twelve now – just gone. It was Good Friday 1977. It was just me and my thoughts and God. I've always liked Easter – a nice civilized celebration in a nice time of the year. There was no one there but us and a young Kevin Lynch was on altar boy duties – making an awful bad fist of lighting candles that weren't supposed to be lit – half a box of matches used up and only one candle firing. I always thought he'd have made a good altar boy – but no, I was wrong – the world's worst.

I decided to talk to God, now that I had the time, but this time – really talk to him. If he wasn't listening of a Good Friday – he might as well give up the day job and become a Protestant – he'd make some Protestant. I asked him the usual stuff first – the personal requests – and then I began to think of the bigger picture. I closed my eyes and I let him have exactly what was on my mind.

"Dear God, you seem to know what's best and that's fair enough – but why is it always so dark and dreary? Is there not some way you could let in... even a small chink of light? Every Sunday we come here – and every Holy Day – we're here at Christmas and Easter – Christenings, Communion, Confirmation, marriages and funerals – and we pray – but very little happens us in between, apart from getting

hardship and a bit closer to the grave! Did you lose your colouring pencils? It's all so dull and grey and poorly lit. What must we do to get colour and light?" Well, I might as well have been talking to myself – when I opened my eyes, Drumeela Chapel was how I had left it – still and peaceful and almost empty – my Mother and Geraldine sat over on the women's side – Margaret, a few seats back – my Father, in his usual spot – Kevin, over from him. There was just us, all strewn around and about and yet we were here together. And although I didn't hear anything – God must have coughed or said something, because suddenly the penny dropped. I was so lucky and I didn't know it. Here I was – like Kevin Lynch above on the alter – struggling and fumbling with matches – trying to light candles that didn't need to be lit.

And then John McCarron came in with his 'post morning stress syndrome' – looking like a cross between a giraffe and a meerkat – long steps, darting stares and gauldering like a Christmas turkey. He used some expletives to sum up what he saw and we all smiled – my whole family in unison – smiling – this was our colour – our light... and all in our own time.

CHAPTER 28

Micky McAweeney

Mickey Mac was like no other – in a valley of mis-fits and oddities – he still stood out. He was in his sixties, a face of lumps and carbuncles and a pair of dancing, watery eyes. He would have fitted very nicely into a Charles Dickens tale. He lived with his brother Frank. Frank had a stick and a limp – we never found out which one he got first. He carried his stick as if he was carrying a weapon. Many's a man he left tracks in – or so he told – we never saw it! All we saw were tracks in the road. He'd bog the metal tip of the blackthorn into the tar, he'd be that vexed. No one there but himself. Falling out with a leftover thought. An after-sting in something McCaffery said in Gorby's the night before. He was fond of Gorby's 'Auld' Bar – they all were – him and his brother and McCaffery, The Wizard Smith, Young Thomas Galligan that played for Ballinamore. Men, as contrary as they were complacent... complacent with time and friendship. Nothing stood in the way of a 'good spake'

– the more reputations you could tear asunder with a word, the longer your own would hold. Frank had respect in that regard – no better man to go searching in your past for a lousy act or betrayal – he'd skip a generation or two, if he thought he could curl your toes with a jibe. He had rolls of money too, *"No damn doubt about it"*, he'd say as he took out the roll of notes to reaffirm his stature and point of view. Didn't like spending it though. Some said there was only currency on the outer layer.

Micky was different. Just as cantankerous, but Micky was more soft-hearted. He wasn't like the others. Most of these other men were bachelors – men who never had to wash themselves for anything other than their wake and funeral. Men who never had to rely on anyone, till their itch became a fester. Micky McAweeney had been married – had a daughter, Kathleen. The wife died young and his daughter went away, but not before they half salvaged some part of him, drew out a sanctified puss, that left him vulnerable, open and warm – albeit erratic – and beneath the roughest exterior imaginable was an empathetic centre – at best, he was like smelling your own fart – when not at his best and he often wasn't – he was like smelling his fart.

I liked Micky Mac – of course I would – and he liked me. He looked like I felt, all bile and blister and my youth and thrust was not unlike his inner self. Micky always helped with our hay and we helped him – that was the way back then. He had no way of doing anything – Daddy had a tractor, a mowing-arm and two strong and willing sons. Micky loved watching us work. He'd be in the kinks of laughter, when me and Kevin would take into one of our flitters of hay-making – piling hay into cocks or hand-shakings – devouring row after row. *"Be God, no worries of a flood with these pair a boyos"*.

In the summer of '77, we thought we were great – a second under 14 championship under our belts and a new milking machine set up in the new byre. The Auld Fella was in his element, enjoying the technology and the help – we were now well used to the work and the dullness. Kevin had decided he was finished with school, he'd be fifteen in September and legally at an age to stop or not start another year – the lucky so-and-so. I had finished my first year, but was only twelve – so I'd have to soldier on, on my own. Margaret was gone to Ballinamore school to do her Leaving Cert and Geraldine was only gone nine. My father was toying with the idea of buying a digger – like a JCB, but smaller – for stubbing whins and rootin'.

He told us this one evening as we stood in one of our reclaimed fields at 'Ginny's Turn' in Druminchin. We had stayed for a minute, admiring our work, before we went home for the tea. A new digger – would that mean less work or more? At the time, it was all work. A few weeks of picking stones helps take the buzzin' out of your bell-bottoms. Daddy stood there outlining his plans to reclaim the countryside – when a jeep went by.

That was very like Jeff Watson's jeep. There weren't many jeeps back then and that was the fifth or sixth time today it had went past.

Daughty Moore had died a few years before – too much time with the egg-man or so McCaffery said – but McCaffery would have took her eggs too, if she had let him. Daughty had failed away to nothing and then died. She was buried in Drumeela and few stood with her after. Her little house was put up for sale and a strange man with a moustache and a family bought it and was going to do it up. He was Watson, he come from South Africa or Zambia or somewhere like that – some said he was from the Isle of Man or English. He never made us any the wiser – the woman was from out foreign too and two childer our age. They had a caravan parked below at the house and he drove about in a big Land Rover – no one knew what he was up to. The wife was a nice woman – couldn't drive – used to come up to our house for milk – started buying milk from us – mostly came up for the company and him in the town drinking.

Jeff Watson was supposed to be a judge at one time, but he had no time for our law – got in with McCaffery and the McAweeneys. He used to bring them to Gorby's in the jeep and Ballinamore or Carrigallen. McCaffery and the McAweeneys would have to be shipped separate as they didn't get on – never spoke, from the day one of them said something to the other and that was it. That happened a good bit back then. Someone would take offence over a word or a few words and from then on, the two parties would only communicate through auld sideways guff, passed on via a third or fourth party – usually standing or sitting sideways at a counter. Good relationships got ruined with spite and then pride.

There was talk at the time, that Watson was a spy – sent over by the English to gather 'intelligence' – if ever a word was out of place... He was an arrogant man – thought he could swan in and charm the locals and he did – to a point. The ones who drank and went to town, they all had good time for him. He was decent, they said – always stood his round – brought them there and home – came in for tea and whatever was going. But he was, 'a bit of a buck', someone else said – said he wasn't an English spy at all – said he was just English and that was worse.

It was the early seventies and although our wee corner of the island was largely unaffected by The Troubles – it didn't mean you could flaunt an English moustache about the place and snort snuff – and the nice woman at home in the caravan with the two childer, dragged to Leitrim against their will – or so they said. There was no sign of him to do up Daughty's cottage and no one knew what he did for money. He had got some grant to start making fibreglass furniture, but that fell through and then he was gone. Supposed to have got a job, 'judging' out in the Seychelles. McCaffery and the McAweeneys were devastated with no lift, but that was it. His wife and kids hung on till they got an opportunity to move to Dublin and then they came up one day and said their goodbyes. Mammy was lonesome after Mrs. Watson and Mammy didn't get lonesome often – they stayed in touch and still do.

But that was years ago – what was his jeep doing back? The next thing Micky McAweeney comes sloping over the road.

"He's back, be God - did ya see the yoke? Watson is back, he mustn't have murdered your man in Oldcastle or stole the gunpowder! They say he started a military coup in the place he was in. There'll be a spree in Gorby's tonight! Ya made a great job of this field, Jim!"

My father picked up on the latter, *"Aye, it turned out not too bad".*

It turned out that the jeep wasn't that of Jeff Watson, just a jeep that looked like it. No one heard from him after and Micky went back to calling him a murderer and a thief, all of which was pub talk and imaginings. Our world thrived on speculation – suckled from it and from it came lots of theories and conjecture. Some colour for our landscape.

Micky Mac stood with us that evening, looking out at the road where the jeep had passed – turned out the jeep belonged to the forestry crowd – someone local was thinking of selling their land for forestry. It wasn't the done thing back then. Daddy thought that would be a sin. Here we were after breaking our backs, to claw back our land from the whins and whitethorns – proud as victors after a match in Croke Park and to think someone would let in the forestry after all that. Micky understood it too – got into one of his emotional states.

"Be God, I never thought I'd see the day, a five-acre field at 'Jinny's Turn' – You're a powerful man, Jim Rourke and ya have two powerful sons – I never seen the leck. And they do tell me in Ballinamore, that we have no land – only scraub – I've a mind to put them on one of 'Martins Buses' and bring them out to see this. I'd take a picture of it, if I could. I'd take pleasure in rubbin' their noses in it. This is what the auld people fought for – this is what they're fighting for up above - with their bombs and their gelignite – hold on tight, Jim Rourke to your land and your sons. You have the greatest gift that God could give – standing in this field".

We always laughed at how Micky said things; said he used to say things arse-ways – start in the middle of a story and tell to both ends – but what he said today, made perfect sense. I knew this land wasn't for me, but I knew it was in good hands and that, come hell or high water – it would never again be let grow over – or taken over by scavengers.

CHAPTER 29

Head Banging

Without a bathroom, it's hard to doll yourself up – we used the scullery as a wash house. We'd put our feet into the old Belfast sink and give them a good scrub – that got rid of most of the smell, although it was hard to differentiate between the smell off our feet and that coming from the six pairs of wellingtons that were kept in the same scullery. My feet were the worst, of course they were. As a teenager, I was inclined to sweat.

I was in second year at the Tech, probably my best year. I had a bit of confidence left over from the summer and for the first time I was on my own. Kevin had quit and Margaret was in Ballinamore. I was real tall now and playing good football – the next big step was the school Hop in the Community Hall – a disco in it's loosest form. I had no interest in going – another pressure cooker for hormonal learner drivers. The thought of reversing a young one around the hall for a half an hour might do it for some, but not for me. I had

seen the older couples sneaking off into the bushes for...
whatever you do in the bushes. I wanted some of that,
but I could never talk to girls – say the right thing – I
could never work out what they were thinking – if they
were thinking at all. Most of them just seemed satisfied
with being lovely. It didn't help that I was a bit of a
romantic – wanting to be like they were in the films on
the telly. I hadn't been to the cinema yet, so I had only
seen musicals on television and 'The Towering Inferno'.
I had a lassie out dancing one time and I said, *"You
dance beautifully"*. I knew the minute I said it, I was on
the wrong continent. She walked off – said I was a
pervert and I didn't know whether I was or I wasn't,
because I had never heard the word before. That's how
bad I was at my best and this was my maiden voyage.

Of course, I had no clothes, only my good clothes. I
looked like I was going to Mass – and the auld soft water
out of the tank had made my hair go all puffy and it hung
down over my eyes – I looked like I was wearing a wig
that was too big for me. If it was a Halloween disco
where everyone dressed up, I might have some chance,
but this was at the time when no one wore a costume to
a Halloween Hop – I just looked like I was going to
Mass. Margaret wasn't going to the Tech anymore, but
she was going to the tonight.

There was a strange atmosphere in the house that
evening. Kevin wouldn't go, I didn't want to go and
Margaret couldn't go unless someone else went. She
cornered me and got around me as usual and promised
to make a tape for me off the radio and what could I do,

other nor go. Michael Lee was going to bring us in and the Auld Fella would bring us home. Margaret washed and ploshed in the scullery for an hour and came out, no better than she went in – she had her hair tied up with a hair band and she didn't even look like herself. She was happy though – this was her first big night out too and her sixteen. I didn't spend as long in the scullery – I had the hair washed from earlier and so I gave myself the cats lick and went upstairs and put on my good clothes. Margaret was in her room singing into a hair brush and getting ready. So, I knelt down at the bed and asked God for guidance. As it turned out, his experience of Carrigallen school hops left a lot to be desired. I prayed:

"Dear God, I don't want to dance with anyone, but I better – Don't let me get giddy, like I sometimes do, when there's a crowd and I promise I'll pray every night next week. Keep Margaret safe from terrorists – Amen".

Margaret was the only bit of the prayer that worked – not one terrorist came near her the whole night – John McCabe asked her how she liked the heavy steel – he meant metal. She was dancing with him because it was near the end and she wanted to dance with someone – it was all heavy metal at that stage, because of the Killashandra ones. John got mixed up between the genre of music and the steel fabrication that was going on below in Newtown. He said, *"How do you like the heavy steel?"*. She said it was alright... if you had a forklift. That didn't confuse John one little bit – he was a grown-up version of me, he was just trying to find a higher gear.

I couldn't get started when I went in first. I hadn't talked to any girls in first year and that wouldn't have helped – I tried a few – asked them to dance – but they pretended they didn't hear me and I pretended I hadn't asked. It was probably the big jumper and the hair that put them off. The bell-bottoms I had from my Confirmation were still trendy, but a good few inches too short. Mammy had threatened to sew a bit to them, but I asked her to hold off till after the hop – maybe that was a bad idea. In spite of all my prayers, the music was making me giddy – The Bee Gee's belted out early on. I kept thinking, 'What would the Auld Lad think of this?'. Mick Duignan and Eamon Daly were keeping control, but they weren't spoiling anyone's night. I'd say, if you took the Killashandra's out of it – most would have been just as wooden and naïve as me.

Then there was a slow-set and the buzzing started up again in my trousers – a smattering of beginners were doing a few very rigid rounds of the floor –nothing like the Killashandra's, when they took into snogging and smooching in front of the teachers. I was getting very warm, with the hair and the jumper and everything else that was going on. The slow set fizzled out and then after that, they rocked it up a bit – I couldn't help but act the eegit – there was ones head-banging and all of a sudden, the nice soft hair, washed with the tank water came into its own. I didn't know what air-guitar was until I was in my twenties, but that must have been what we were at, that first night in Carrigallen. I was just copying everyone else. I was out of my tree with buck-lepping and noise – Margaret saw what I was at and must have decided I was a lost cause. She went off outside with Mary Lee to wait for our lift. I couldn't stop myself from getting carried away with the music – then there was a bit of horse-play – some of the Killashandra's started leaping into me and I stuck out me chest and let them at it – I thought I was the toughest, coolest kid on the block, but I wasn't. I had a big red face from the pressure of the uncoordinated, whip-lash provoking torture that was head-banging. Even my hair had a headache. Our Vice Principle, Eamon Daly stuck in a restraining arm at one point and like a boxing referee – pulled me back from the hotbed of the dancefloor. He was careful with his words.

"Take it easy, Seamie – you've already invented a dozen new dance moves – give the Killashandra's a chance to catch up. Save your energy for the football field."

There was always an assumption that white men from Drumeela couldn't dance. I had just turned that assumption into fact.

I retired to a place of calm and tried to digest my madness. I suddenly felt vulnerable and shy again. The music stopped abruptly, as if I had broken it with my misguided energy. Then they played the National Anthem. I stood – a fine embodiment of youth – that's what I should have been – but I was just the biggest balooba in the smallest of community halls. I grabbed what was left of my dignity and went outside.

It was so difficult being a teenager, or it was at the time. When you're big, people expect more of you – expect you to act like someone of your size, but not your age. I always stood out – I wanted to stand out, but I wanted to fit in even more and I didn't, how could I and the state of me? I caught my reflection in a car window. I looked like my mother knitted me – hair and all. Micky Lee came out then – I got some comfort from seeing him – he looked like a tall bottle of fizzy lemonade in 'heat'. His cork was about to pop. He had picked up the scent of several *'chancy enough ones'* and was anxious to share this bounty with me. I wouldn't know what to do with a chancy one, if she fell into my lap. I wanted to go home.

The Auld Fella pulled up in the middle of the street in front of the hall. What was he thinking of? Why didn't he go down to the handball alley to turn or we could have discreetly met him somewhere else, instead of drawing attention to himself and us and his silly farmer's cap. Daddy always wore a cap – to let everyone know that we were farmers and that we hadn't a clue about anything. Margaret sat in the passenger seat and me and the Lees squished into the back – thankfully I got buried beneath a load of bodies and didn't have to look out.

When I got into bed that night, I was exhausted and the buzzing had moved to my head. Micky Lee was right – the disco was too loud. I lay there replaying the evening in slow motion. I knew St Patrick was looking down with that big disappointed look of his and I was trying to work out why. What had I done wrong? I couldn't find one positive thought to lure me to sleep. All I could see, were people laughing at me – my hair, my jumper, by bell-bottoms – what parents in their right mind would let their child choose bell-bottoms for their Confirmation? Why did my mother and father spend the last twelve years minding me – protecting me – pulling me out of bog-holes – only to throw me into a social setting, where I almost drowned. Were it not for Eamon Daly, I could have been savaged by Killashandra's. I was on my own with them for half an hour... on the dancefloor – there was no sign of Micky Lee and his entourage of chancy ones, when the Killashandra's were launching into me during 'Smoke on the Water'! And there was no sign of God there either. God had let me down – again. I hadn't felt the power of the Holy Spirit one little bit since Confirmation. Surely things had to get better.

CHAPTER 30

The Outsider

A t school, I was one of the biggest wasters going. When I started the Tech in Carrigallen, I set down a marker and I stuck by it. The only problem is, the marker was put down in the first few days, when I hadn't got a clue. My plan for government was made within minutes of me getting off the bus that first morning – and it was... to be an eegit. I was going to be as thick and as unproductive as possible for as long as possible... and I was. I contributed nothing in class, even if I knew something, I didn't let on; if I found myself becoming interested in a topic – I quickly found distraction and with it, disruption. I was on a crash-course of defiance and detention. I avoided the studious and befriended the indifferent – any individual with delusions of development, were hacked down at the knees and ostracized.

I was now in a gang – a gang of two, me and Kevin Martin – we were the boys – anti-establishment – antilearning – anti-everything except Aunty Peggy... she sent Birthday cards with money.

Kevin Martin was from Killashandra, but wasn't a townie... he was country with the swagger of a townie. He came from a big family and was somehow, a slightly more developed version of me... or so I thought. We hung around in our very exclusive gang and stuck our fingers up to anything that moved in a positive direction. Kevin was older and so I was going to lose him at the end of second year – he would be fifteen by then and that was him – gone – but we made the most of what time we had.

We were late for every class and were gone before every bell. We sang dumb for every question, yet had a smart remark for every lull. The teachers must have hated us, but never gave us the satisfaction of letting us know. We were a pathetic pair – swanning around, thinking we were the boys. Heading off down the town whenever we felt like it or smoking in the 'Dales' (a cluster of trees beside the pre-fabs).

Kevin was into everything that didn't involve school. He couldn't wait to get away. He said his life would begin, the minute he left. I envied him – I just went about with my 'I'm going to play for Leitrim' head on me. We didn't have proper conversations – we were stand-in company for each other while we were at school, like prison mates. All bluff and blunder on the outside – totally insecure within. But we weren't going to change.

Mick Duignan and Mr. Daly came into our class one day with good news or at least good news as they saw it. Ours was the first class at the school, who could complete their full secondary education. The school would, from 1981, incorporate the Leaving Cert. Up until then, students could only do first, second and third year – and then move to another school, to do the Leaving Certificate or stay for a fourth year in Carrigallen to do 'Pre Employment' (for boys) or 'Secretarial Year' (for the girls) – a handy, mostly practical year getting us ready for the workplace. There was also an option at the time to skip third year and go directly from second year to Pre-Employment – which I intended to do.

Now they had the Leaving Cert and everyone was very excited – well not everyone. It's always worrying when a lot of people get excited at the same time – mass hysteria over an extra exam – the goody-goodies were beside themselves – the rest of us couldn't give a damn.

The Powers That Be were not too happy, when only six out of our class said they would stay on to do the Leaving Cert. This was bad news – six out of thirty-six – there was going to be pressure on to encourage more. I'd stick my heels in the ground. Eamon Daly approached me one day about the matter.

"Damn it all Seamie, you're bright and intelligent – why not channel that in a positive direction? No one's saying you have to be an academic. You have so many talents – for woodwork, metalwork – you're developing as a sports man and a person..."

I looked around to see who he was talking to. I hated a lecture from Mr. Daly – it was always so civil – he always had your future at heart. I'd far rather get a good haymaker from Mr. Duignan – it was easier to withdraw and sulk after a good slap. Daly just talked to you as an equal – made you feel bad for being a Ninny-Hammer. I ended up telling him I'd think about it – I had no intention of thinking about anything.

In order to do the Leaving Cert, I'd have to do four more years – I was already twelve – that would mean I wouldn't be finished school until I was sixteen – no way – I'd rather be a Ninny-Hammer any day.

Coming up to Christmas '77, the school was having an annual concert in No2 – each year would put a few acts together and compete in a nice friendly non-competitive way. Our year had a meeting and there were suggestions that me and Kevin Martin do some sort of double act – we were always quick with our smart jibes – how about some comedy? I was intrigued – the idea floored my mate – I could see the genuine fear in his eyes when I said, *"Maybe we should give it a try"*. I wanted to do it, mostly, because I thought he was hilarious – but, no way was he going down that road. I didn't come up with anything in particular, but I kept thinking of the school's reaction if we were to nail a wee comedy routine. He was adamant – no way would the school get him. Still, there was something inside of me that was desperate to take part and I hung around when the others were practicing. A few times, I was asked to step in, but I just gave them a shrug of indifference and sauntered off down 'Nowhere Street'. I was afraid they'd laugh at me – I was afraid they wouldn't laugh at me – I was just afraid. I'm sure no one remembers that concert or the build-up to it, but I do and there was more to come.

The Tech is just out the Mohill road from the village of Carrigallen. As you walk from the school back towards the small cluster of houses and businesses, the Town Lake is on the right, after that a row of tiny houses backing on to the lake – the first of these was 'McHugh's Sweetshop' – an oasis of Club Orange and Catch Bars. Mrs. McHugh was a lady and always had a smile and an interest in who was who – her husband Joe, came out of the kitchen when things got busy, but always looked out of place in the shop. In summer we bought ice-cream and minerals and in winter, we stuffed ourselves with bars and crisps. Some of us mightn't have survived school without McHugh's shop or McManus's, below at the corner. On this day in early December, as we returned from lunchbreak down town, Mr. Daly was on the road, as usual – minding us – making sure we didn't get knocked down or abducted. He hovered about on his hovercraft platforms – like John Lennon directing traffic in Jerusalem – his hippy hair dancing and darting about like he had just bathed in the soft waters of a rain barrel. The farmers on their way to the cattle mart, turning back for a second look. *'Who is yer man with the hair?'*

This day, Eamon took me to one side – for once, I wasn't doing anything wrong – he asked me about the concert – would I not join in the sketch? – but that wasn't his main objective. He wanted me to think about my future – do the Leaving Certificate and it would stand to me. I thought it was as good a time as any to let him know my plans. I said I was going to finish second year and then slip nice and quietly into fourth year and when I had completed my pre-employment year – I was for the high-road. He was very disappointed, but left it at that.

Me and my brother could eat spuds for Ireland – that evening at the dinner table, we were in full flow – the six of us sat around a saucepan of boiled potatoes and a chop and we got stuck in. The levels of concentration at our dinner table were way ahead of any commitment given to school or worship – we'd eat our way through any crisis or storm. It was Mammy noticed the Volkswagen Beetle coming up the lane; she was always on the look-out for 'bloody visitors'. The car was familiar – it belonged to Eamon Daly – panic ensued – our house could only receive 'important' visitors after my mother had a three minute fit – no attempt was made to tidy – these three minutes were for hiding stuff – torn coats, dirty towels, buckets, pet pigs, calf-powders and any other signs of poverty. The saucepan from the middle of the table was fired into the scullery – still half-full of spuds – me and Kevin were raging. No one seemed to care what the principle and vice-principle of my school might be coming for – it was all about the presentation and how we looked to them when they got here.

The two men had tea – and cake – wherever the Auld Lassie got the cake from? We hadn't had cake for months and all of a sudden – here it was on a china plate. The men broached the subject of me skipping into fourth year without doing my Inter Cert. It turns out, I would only be fourteen at the end of pre-employment and not legally entitled to quit school or legally entitled to take up a job. That was bullshit – lots had quit at thirteen and fourteen – but they said the law was now much more strict – I'd have to do third year – and maybe after that, I might consider doing the Leaving Cert. Oh yea – and stay at school till I was an old man (of sixteen). Of course, I didn't vent my anger, just sang dumb in the corner – but no one else said anything either. Here was my life hanging by a thread and all my parents asked, was, did they want any more tea? And then they left and the cake was put away.

There was no discussion after they had gone – only relief that the teachers hadn't spotted the mouse, who had come in to hear some of the big words. I decided there and then, that was me finished with school. I couldn't quit, but I wasn't going to co-operate in any way. I took every book out of my bag and for the next two and a half years – I would only bring my lunch to school. I don't know what I wanted my parents to say, but I wanted them to say something – to take sides – to have an opinion, but decent country people didn't argue with teachers or priests or doctors – they just gave them tea and cake.

Life at school was different after that. I was more determined than ever to do nothing – yet I couldn't help but become interested in some of the information that was floating about. I tried hard to quench my inquisitiveness by concentrating on football and going down town – soon Kevin Martin's indifference was no match for mine.

At the Christmas Concert, we watched and disrupted like a pair of grouches in the box-seats of a Muppet Show. We thought we were great – Statler and Waldorf – but all we really were, was pathetic. Our year won the prize for their endeavours – they gleefully accepted a big box of chocolates and headed off to classroom No 6 to celebrate. Me and Kevin Martin thought it would be rude not to join them and grab a fistful of sweets for ourselves.

I will always remember the look on their faces, when we walked in. We had not been part of their journey – we had mocked and avoided the pressure of getting up before an audience. While they were practicing, we were down town scrounging crisps. We were not available when the graft and commitment was required. Now that the graft had turned to glory – we were not wanted.

I learned one of the biggest lessons of my life that day. Be part of it – whatever it is – don't hang around on the outside – get in there. And don't ever disrespect human endeavour. Regardless of talent or ability – anyone who puts in time and effort are way above those who scoff and hide. Always be on the honest side – the inside – where the wheels get shifted and turned – where mistakes happen and get repaired – where vulnerability gradually turns to confidence and magic is forged not found.

It was only a school concert – the prize was only a box of 'Milk Tray', but whatever pleasure and satisfaction it brought – it was in Room No 6 that day. Me and Kevin Martin missed out on it and slinked off in our two-man gang. He didn't care. He wasn't into that sort of thing, but I was and it hurt. There is no substitute for being part of something and simply doing your best.

CHAPTER 31

Flashes

I sat in the passenger seat of the Escort – waiting – my mother was in the driver's seat. If you were outside the car, you wouldn't know she was there – she was still adjusting the seat and putting in cushions and Lego bricks to get her head up over the dash. It was the Summer of '78, I was thirteen. Tomás Mimna had told me he was getting a summer job in McCartin's Engineering down in Newtowngore. That got me going – I had to get a job there too. I decided I needed the money – I wasn't sure what for, but it was no harm having some. If nothing else, it would get me out of the meadow. The prospect of being a working man was inviting. Who would I ask about the job? I could ask Tom Mimna, to ask for me. Tom worked there, I'm sure it was him got Tomás the job. No, I'll not annoy him with that. I'll go straight to the top. I'll get my mother to drive me down to one of the McCartin houses and I'll ask myself.

Mammy had started to drive. Up until that she never went anywhere – partly because she had nowhere to go, but also she had never learned to drive the car. She could drive the tractor – in a sort of a way. She sat on it, as if she was sitting on an uncontrollable animal – expecting it to bolt at any moment. She paired all her actions with a constant, high pitched whinny, which only added to the terror. Because she was pocket-size – she had to slide off to either side in search of a clutch or break – she was never quite sure which was which. She hated driving the tractor and only did, under severe duress. My mother was now thirty-six – she had four kids between ten and seventeen – life now was a doddle. It was – compared to what had gone before.

When my grandfather was alive and living with us and my father had taken on the evening shift in McCartin's Mill, back in the early '70's – my mother was at full throttle. She recalled one evening, there was a bit of wind forecast. My mother and father had just cocked the big meadow in Killerin – there were thirty-six stacks of hay that needed tying down. That morning, Mammy had milked the thirteen cows by hand – fed the calves – got three of us ready for school – her four children were between nine and two. During the day, she knitted and picked blackcurrants – she had bought a load of blackcurrant bushes, so she could make jam to sell. We got back from school at four and she had our dinner ready – she made her husband's lunch and at five, he went to work. She then milked the thirteen cows again – on her own and did the things and after milking, she headed for Killerin on the bike. She left me and my sister with our grandfather and she put Margaret on the carrier and Kevin on the handle-bars and cycled the mile or so down to the hay – there she headed the thirty-six cocks. She trimmed the butts – pointed the heads and tied two ropes on each one and then at twenty-past-eleven that night, she was finished. My father picked them up on his way from work. He put the bike in the boot and the hay was saved from wind and storm.

My mother thought nothing of this – this was what had to be done – driving a car was a different proposition altogether. The driver's seat of the Escort was low – the Auld Lad had it destroyed with constant prizing himself in and out of it. There was always a folding match, when the Auld Fella sat into a car. Six-foot-three inches of knees and elbows. Mammy was five-foot-two and didn't fold. The first thing she needed, was a cushion or two – Mammy's many cushions – they brought her up, just above the steering wheel and still low enough for her feet to touch the pedals. She was stretched to the limit. She clung to the steering at ten to two – every action was matched with a prayer. She and Jesus have shared the driving for over forty years. She failed her first driving test, because she was nervous and still running into things. By the time her second one came around – they had cleared the road and she rallied home with a clear round.

Mammy drove me to Newtown that day. We went to Tommy McCartin's house, but there was no one there

– we then went to his brother, Joe's house. I got out and knocked – I asked his wife if he was about and he came. I was thirteen and yet I knew when I met Joe McCartin for the first time, that I was in the company of a great man. My father had huge respect for these two brothers – but I knew from the first moment we met, that there was something about him. He was busy and businesslike – he was pleasant, but not condescending – he was very interested in who I was and I told him and I told him what I wanted – a summer job. He asked me my age – I lied – I said I was fifteen. He said I was a big fifteen, but then my father was a big man. He told me to come down the following Monday and we'd get started. Mammy couldn't take in my news, as she was trying to man the Escort into return mode. She was more on for talking to the man above, than she was to me. They got us home and then she said, *"Now tell me"* – I said:

> *"He said I could start Monday"*
> *"Did he ask what age you were?"*
> *"He did – I said fifteen"*
> *"What else would you say? How are you going to get there?"*
> *"I could go on the bike"*
> *"Or you could ask Tom"*

Tom Mimna was a foreman in the Engineering – he drove a forklift and was a foreman in the yard. He and Tomás would be going past our lane every morning. I went up and asked Tom and he was more than willing to give me a lift.

On Monday morning, I was getting ready for my first day at work – my wardrobe for such an event was sparse. I had grown out of most of my clothes except my trusty bell-bottoms – Mammy had sewed a few inches to the bottom of them and although I couldn't wear them to Mass, due to the slight variation in colour, they would be ideal for work – apart from the fact that each leg was about eighteen inches wide and I was going to be working around steel and sharp edges, but these were all I had. My mother made a tamp of sandwiches and put them in an empty biscuit tin, along with two spoonfuls of loose tea in a jar – sugar, in another jar and a bottle of milk in a Salad Cream bottle – and I was now an official member of the Lunch-box Union – bound for the Engineering.

Tom had a green Volkswagen Beetle – he picked me up at the bottom of the lane and me, him and Tomás headed for Mullyaster. As we drove up the hill towards the McCartin empire – I could see the piggery on the left; the Mill, where daddy had worked, on the right and ahead was our destination – the Engineering. At the time there were fifty working at the place. Everyone clocked in, but no sign of my name on a card just yet. It was a real factory atmosphere. Steel Fabrication was the business, but no one knew who was in charge. There were the McCartins themselves – then a general manager – then another manager or two – then a foreman and another foreman – then there were those who took it on themselves to supervise everyone else, including management and then there was me – at the bottom of the pile – of course I was.

There were games of cards in the mornings, cards at breaktime and then at lunchtime, everyone spilled out into the yard, where the employees of the engineering took on the boys from the mill and piggery in a game of – well, there was no name for this game – it was a game with no rules.

There were two sets of goalposts and a ball, but no other rules... apart from – if someone got cut on the steel or broke their leg, the game was stopped till they got out of the way. It was no place for a boy in bell-bottoms – but a great place to prove yourself to be a man... and I did.

On the factory floor, I was hell-bent on making an impact and proving I was a worthy employee – my eagerness was soon exploited. Any bit of lifting or donkey work that had to be done, I was called for and I took great delight in abusing myself at every opportunity. I raced from one hazardous task to the next, bounding over girders and cleats, catching my flairs and getting flashed by welders from every corner. Tom Mimna kept telling me to settle myself – that they were only making a cod of me, but I kind of knew that anyway. This was more for me – to prove to myself, that I had it in me to survive in the big bad world. The work wasn't a problem. At the time, myself and Kevin were fit for any type of physical challenge. We spent our spare time hoisting hundred weights of cement over our heads; doing press-ups and chin-ups; wrestling weanling calves and lifting small tractors – physically not a problem. No – my only problem was the paint and the weld flashes. When it was time to go home, Tom had to put a sheet of plastic on the seat of the Volkswagen, as I was smeared in red paint and black from smoke fumes.

The Auld Fella said I must have let them walk all over me – literally. I thought I had done well. Me and the Auld Fella's measuring sticks were becoming out of sync. That night the welder's flash really took hold. I didn't know what was happening – first I thought my eyes were full of sand – then I genuinely felt I was going blind. By morning, it was worse, but I was still going to work. I couldn't see much that morning, but I could see the disappointment on my father's face. He was afraid for me and annoyed with himself for not warning me. He tried to give me a crash-course in how not to be an eegit, but I wasn't listening – I had the course half completed. That morning, there was a card for me to clock in – it was now official – I was on the payroll. Two weeks into the job, I got my first cheque - £10 – everyone went to Gerald Johnston's shop in Newtown to get their cheques cashed. Tom drove us there. I queued with the rest, got my cash. There's no end to the amount of sweets you can buy for a tenner.

CHAPTER 32

The War Hero

I was togging out at the back of the National School in Carrigallen – it was a Friday evening and we had under 14 football. I was coming from work in the Engineering and covered in black dust and red paint that looked like blood. My flared trousers were patched and torn. I was like a war hero coming back from the trenches. I was also a shocking size for me age. The new under 14 team stood around watching me. We had won two under 14 championships while I was eleven and twelve and most of that team were now over age – I was the only one still eligible to play – in fact I had this year and next. The lads standing around me, watching me tog out were very young and very small. I was towering over everyone and I hated it. I didn't mind the responsibility of being captain – I looked forward to the elevated status. It's just, I wanted to blend in more. But, I was turning up for training in my work clothes – these fellas were just out of nappies.

My father had been a founder member of the new juvenile club in Carrigallen. He wasn't directly involved with the under 14's, but he was preparing the runway for my crash-landing. This team was going from – the team who had won everything – to the team nobody wanted to know. He'd say, *"It was great to get the two good years – when Brian Brady was winning matches on his own, but there's only one Brian Brady."* There was no disputing what he was saying – he was right – he was always right. No man talked more sense than Jim Rourke. When it came to stating the obvious – my old man was king. But that was no use to me. My father's world was lived out in hard facts – if I didn't have my dreams and imaginings – I couldn't survive. Too many people insist on stating the obvious – giving you a good jerk back down to reality – telling you what you can't do and why you shouldn't try. These people are often afraid that you might succeed and leave them behind, but my father wasn't one of them. He was just afraid for me and the consequence of failure.

On that Friday evening at the school field, I was ready. The team were gathered in the open shed at the back of the school. Because I was from out Drumeela way, I didn't know some of my new teammates – they looked like they came out of a tin – like sardines. The smallest, scrawniest little fellas. I had seen bigger giblets coming out of a turkey at Christmas. I knew by our trainer, the postman – John Donnelly, that he didn't hold out much hope either – he spent most of his time gazing up into the field, where the new Junior team were training. *"It's great to see adult football back in this parish – I never thought I'd see the day"* and it was great – I thought it was great – but this was under 14's and we needed to get started. Someone mentioned that we were going for three-in-a-row. *"Three-in-a-row - my granny"*, our trainer said. All he talked about, was the loss of our star players and *"Don't get in the way of the Juniors"*. I decided to show leadership. I grabbed the ball – everyone was now looking in awe at the Juniors. I said, *"Come on lads – one day, that will be us!"* I was a foot taller than everyone else, including the postman. I ran towards the low fence and the little gate that separated the school grounds from the sports field and I thought about jumping it – I had seen lads jump it – but I decided to tear through the gate instead and I did – with such power and determination, that the gate swung back and flattened three of my gosling teammates. I didn't notice till I heard them crying in a heap behind me. So much for three-in-a-row – I had to go back and apologise – I saw the look of disappointment in John Donnelly's eyes. All I could say was sorry.

When we were small, we were always sent to bed early – there was nothing of interest for us on the television after 8 o'clock. If some of the neighbours didn't come for cards – it was a long night in the house with just us. The Auld Lad read the paper and Mammy would knit or make jam – anything other than sit down and do nothing. As we got older, we stayed up longer and watched more telly. I was now taking a great interest in 'Wonder Woman' and any programme with a bit of flesh in it. I'm sure my brother was too, but I can only vouch for myself. At the time I thought there was something wrong with me. I was at an age where even the sight of 'Little-Bo-Peep' on the label of 'Laird's Bo-Peep Jam' was getting me aroused. We didn't buy Laird's Bo-Peep Jam – but Mammy secretly collected empties from the dump in the bog for her jam – sometimes the label was still on – or half torn – even sexier. Mammy was always making jam.

One week, the Mid-Week Movie was 'Ryan's Daughter' with Robert Mitchum and Sarah Miles – I had never seen a naked breast before and then one came on the telly. I was conscious of my surroundings – the Auld Lad was afraid to look out from behind the Leitrim Observer – he could hear the ridin' music going goodo. Mammy was doing a horrid bit of stirring at the jam – trying to whisk away the danger of me becoming a man right there in front of them. There was no danger of that – our telly was too fuzzy for that. But that breast stayed with me a lifetime – fuzz or no fuzz.

Sarah Miles was a real snake charmer – everything around that time was charming my snake. This led me to believe that I was possessed by something sinful – something dirty. I probably needed another trip to Dr. Farrelly or the priest, but what would they know. Wonder Woman would probably go over their heads - maybe it would go away by itself. But it didn't and there was no one to tell me. There had to be something amiss with me.

The under 14 practice was pathetic – I wasn't allowed to tackle the others, because they kept falling over, some of them still whimpering from when I swung the gate back at them. I kept picking them up, but they kept falling over again – eventually John Donnelly called a halt. He told me to go over to the Juniors – the grown up's – and try knocking them over. I thought he was joking – he wasn't. He thought I'd be delighted to get playing with the adults – I thought I'd be delighted – but I wasn't. I was just embarrassed. I had been thrown out, because I was too big and too clumsy. I had been on the team for two years, but had never really fitted in, because I was too young. Now, nearing the right age – I was too big. I was devastated.

When school started back in September, I was loaded. £10 a week for fourteen weeks. I could head down town at lunchtime with my head held high. It had been a tough summer – I had learned a lot: Cover your eyes in front of welders. Cover your eyes from Sarah Miles'. Sex and welding can blind you. And be careful what you wish for. I was now in third year – I didn't want to be in third year – I had my heart set on fourth year – pre-employment – I had got a taste of commercialism and I was hooked on working for money. I hadn't learned anything as valuable as that in my twelve years so far at school. Now I had to rein in any thoughts of freedom and knuckle down to doing nothing. I had no intention of co-operating in this – my third year at the Tech.

The girls were all lovely at school, even the knock-kneed ones. Maybe this year would be the year I'd try talking to one – but what would we talk about? I'm sure they heard about our disastrous under 14 season – six games played – six hidings. We couldn't talk about school, because I wasn't taking part in school – I had emptied my schoolbag at the end of last year and I was now simply going through the motions. No homework, no study – just traipsing around from one classroom to the next. The teachers would call me up to the blackboard every now and then – get me to solve a problem – trying to catch me out – but I always got away with it – or so I thought. What was I thinking of? Someone who thinks they're great, because they got through school without learning anything! My father would say, *"That's a sure sign of an eegit"*

My father was disappointed in me for not doing my Leaving Cert. He never said that outright, but I knew he was. Maybe he wasn't – I never knew exactly what he was disappointed about, but he always was and I held it against him. Sometime in my early teens – I decided that my father was disappointed with me for everything. I could do nothing right. I wasn't able to do a Brian Brady on the football team – I didn't show the same zest for hardship as my brother or either of my sisters or my mother. I wasn't into books and would never walk on the moon. I had made a very good teapot stand in woodwork class, but that was it. An empty vessel on a really well-made shelf.

As the exams approached in the summer of '79 – I was excited. I was almost finished third year and next year would be my last. I had summer work lined up in McCartin's and my wages were going up by £2 to £12 a week. The exams themselves didn't bother me in the slightest – I'd do what I could and enjoy the sunshine. There was always good weather when the exams were on. During the Inter Cert of '79, the sun shone every day! I'd be halfway through an exam and I'd hear a ball being thumped out in the yard and I'd promptly pack my wisdom in to one final paragraph and head outside to the sunshine and the freedom.

The freedom I felt, when that year was over! The Tech was the makings of me. It will always have a special place in my memory. I learned in spite of myself. I learned mostly about integrity – I gained confidence and strength and one hell of a teapot stand.

CHAPTER 33

Planting Bombs

I never rode a motor-bike. There, I said it; and I had never been in a proper lorry. I wanted to be a lorry driver, so it was time I got in one soon. That time I was fourteen – I went to the Engineering for the summer. The place was flying – the demand for steel fabricated farm buildings was extraordinary. There were sheds being shipped off to as far away as Donegal and Mayo. We started at half eight in the morning – worked till five and then some of us did overtime until nine. Sometimes, someone had to go off on the lorry with a load – that was a real treat – two hours sitting up in a big 'Scania' – twenty minutes work – and then another two hours home. I hadn't got on any of these trips during my first summer, so I made it perfectly clear that I was available and willing this year.

John O'Brien was one of the drivers – a laidback, unassuming man, who had spent a lifetime in England – nothing fazed him – yet. He was in the canteen at tea break – that didn't happen too often – he'd usually be gone first thing, but there was a delay today on a huge shed for the top tip of Donegal. If only I could get that jaunt. As the day progressed, I could see him eyeing me up. Although all the young lads liked to get away on the truck – they also liked getting home early – not me – there was a meadow of hay waiting for me and I'd do anything to get away in a truck. As 4 o'clock approached, the truck was being loaded. Surely he wasn't heading away at this time – then John approached – *"Are you up for a bit of a run?"*, says he. *"I am"*, says I. *"Have you anything else to wear?"*, says he – I was still in my Confirmation flairs. They were well flittered and patched several times and another two inches sewed to the bottom of the two inches that got sewed on last year. I had nothing else to wear, unless I went home and put on my Mass clothes. John said it was just that we'd be stopping somewhere for a bit to eat and we mightn't be let in, if we looked like we were after planting a bomb. He looked again at my trousers and said, *"You look like you've just planted a bomb... and didn't get away on time..."* Then, *"Come on – we'll see how it goes"*. This was great – my first time in the 'Scania' – what a machine. I gave a little smug wave to everyone as we drove out the yard. So, this is what it felt like to drive a lorry. Such a feeling of power and adventure. Come on John – give her the didi!

Our family never went anywhere – we had nearly been to Dublin once. We were all heading off to visit Mammy's aunt and first cousin in Clontarf one time and just outside Navan we hit a patch of oil and the car spun round on the road several times and finished up pointing back for Drumshangore. The car must have known what the Auld Lad would be like driving in Dublin. He wasn't great in built-up areas. He had been around a roundabout once in Enniskillen – he went the wrong way – met a load of cars he didn't know. He broke a red light in Longford another time – he didn't jump it – he ran into it. And now this skid. It was a fierce trauma for us, that had never been in Meath before and here we were doing donuts in front of strangers. A guard came on the scene – how humiliating! That trip was talked about for years – 'The day we took the skid going to Dublin'.

We never went on holidays either – that was not a thing in our house. There might have been one trip to the beach in Bundoran, but no one remembers that – because we didn't get a skid that day. Of course, we never longed for holidays – because we didn't know what we were missing. Our holidays began when the last of the hay was in the shed and there'd come on a skiff of a shower. There is no feeling like it. We didn't need holidays – holidays were for townies and the English. My sister, Margaret had gone to Bundoran to work for the summer, a few years before – the trip bookmarked, by the purchase of an ABBA tape – but that was it – Bundoran twice and Dublin once, but not with the bird's eye view that I had today.

Myself and my fellow trucker, John, pulled up in Buncrana, Co.Donegal – we had finally reached our destination. It was seven in the evening. He backed into a yard – there was no one there to help us unload – everything had to be taken off by hand. This wasn't as tough a task as it sounds, if you had the knack – John O'Brien had the knack. He wasn't a big man, in fact he was slight, but he knew what he was doing. I didn't. I raced about, dancing out of the way of falling trusses and girders – lifting when there was no need to lift – pulling when I should have pushed. When most of the big stuff was unloaded, John and I climbed onto the forty-foot body of the lorry. This was where John's faith in young lads was pushed to the limit.

There were two thirty-foot trusses left on the body, along with all the small stuff – cleats and sharp edges everywhere. I was so keen to help, I lost the run of myself completely. I raced about – catching my patched-up flairs in every cleat and endplate there was. Within a matter of minutes, I was looking like 'The Incredible Hulk' after he'd come out of one of his fits. My bell-bottoms were in ribbons – my white fleshy calves and thighs covered in red paint and scratches. I looked like a ransacked curtain shop and John O'Brien was fuming. He was too nice to say what he was actually thinking – but he did tell me that we wouldn't be stopping anywhere for dinner. He said *"Seamus, my dear young man – I can't bring you in anywhere to eat – I'd be arrested for cruelty. We'll have to stop and get chips somewhere, as long as you stay in the cab"*.

It was after midnight when I got home – my mother was still up – I hadn't told her or sent word that I was going to be late. When she saw me – she thought I had been in an accident. My good trousers hanging off me, my legs covered in paint, blood and ketchup and me – almost asleep. She said to clean myself up. I picked off the rough stuff and went to bed. The next morning, we officially said goodbye to my Confirmation flairs. Mammy took the buttons off and the zip and kept them for spares. Nothing else could be saved. The next Friday week I got my cheque for my efforts – my wages plus three evenings till nine and one till midnight came to just over £40. I was in the money now and only seven more months till I'd be fifteen and a legal age to leave school.

My brother was now playing football with Carrigallen Juniors – the men's team. Towards the end of the summer he was heading off to play a friendly match in Eslin. Padraig Brady called for him and asked me to come along as they might be stuck for numbers. I was at the stage when I'd wear my football togs under my trousers most days. You'd never know when there might be a football match and a chance of a game – you couldn't let anyone see your underwear or lack of it – just for the sake of wearing your togs under your trousers. That evening, I was needed and so made my debut in a bottom field in Eslin.

What was great about playing adults football at fourteen, was that you didn't have to be careful – most of them – not all – but most, were able to take a hit. There wasn't as much time spent picking them up and apologising – trying to get them to stop crying. The football back then was coarse and slow and Carrigallen were big and slow – but there was also a smattering of young lads from the famous under 14 team. Things were looking up for next year. I was put in corner forward – of course I was. I enjoyed it great. All the older lads had nothing but encouragement and praise. What was not to like. I got a few scores and did okay, but I was very aware that it was only a friendly and there was a lot of good will bouncing around. We stopped at the shop on the way home, and I had loads of dosh to buy myself a Coke. I was ready to take on the world.

As September approached, I began to think about the future. Yes, it was great that this was my last year at school, but what happens after that? Where would I get a job? Did I really want to work in the Engineering? The future didn't seem as cut and dried as it once did. When we started back at school – there was a noticeable change. I was now in 'Pre-Employment' and being treated like an adult, this was different and nice and it reminded me that fourth year was real. It was preparing us for employment out in the big bad world.

I soon put the future to one side and began to enjoy the year that was in it. It had all happened very suddenly, but I was now a veteran of the school. Only the teachers had been there longer than me and because of the nature of our course, any odd jobs or small renovations around the place fell into our hands. Suddenly we had responsibility and a new relationship with teacher, principal and caretaker alike. We were doing everything, but teaching classes – or so we thought.

In March 1980 – I began to wonder. I had just turned fifteen – fifteen was the magic number. I could leave school anytime I wanted, but I really didn't want to – I had nowhere to go. The teachers' thoughts were turning to exams – we had no exams – we were no longer centre stage. My former classmates were in a different fourth year – next year, they would be the first students to do the Leaving Cert – that had its attractions – I was at a cross-roads. Then one Sunday at Mass, Sean Brady said his neighbour, Tommy Reilly of the Rough Hill was looking for an apprentice carpenter – to give him a shout. I cycled over the next day – he said I could start at £25 a week. It wasn't lorry driving and it wasn't great money – but it was a job and an apprenticeship – whatever that was worth. He said I could start on Monday-week – the 10th of April – and I said I would.

I went to school the next week to avoid the work at home – I didn't do anything mad – just told them I was leaving on Friday and I did. No young fella had gone as easy on the education system as me to that point. Little did I know – I wasn't entirely finished with it yet.

CHAPTER 34

On Our Bike

On the 10th of April 1980 I cycled the three miles or so to Tommy Reilly's of the Rough Hill – I had a tamp of sandwiches and enough enthusiasm to fight a small war. I fitted in – just about. It was a small workshop with a low ceiling and I was over six-foot-two and an awful spring in me step. I had planned this day for a long time.

I'd had a week to prepare for this new job and after school, I spent most of that time doing up a bicycle that had belonged to my father. I never saw my father ride a bike – he had moved on to driving badly when I met him. We never had bikes as kids. There was one bike that everyone used. It was Mammy's bike – a woman's bike, with no crossbar. It was an embarrassment to be seen riding a woman's bike at the time – the only other alternative was a bike that had been hanging up in the shed this years. This was Daddy's bike – a huge big black thing – it was like getting up on a small horse. It needed doing up – breaks, peddles, tyres and most importantly – and to preserve my coolness – paint. Black paint for a black, flying machine. This would be my trusty steed for the next few years and it had to look presentable. It had no gears or hang-down handle bars, but I could crouch forward and pretend I had those. I scoured Mullan Market for accessories – I thought about go-faster stripes, but decided they were too tacky. I went for a horn instead – a real big horn with a black rubber air egg – that you squeezed when you wanted to let on-coming traffic know that you were approaching. The traffic wouldn't be my biggest problem on my way to the Rough Hill, but still – better to have it, just in case.

The Auld Fella said I was getting up on the bike wrong – of course I was. I was throwing my leg over from a standing position – positioning myself straddle-legged on the saddle – finding the right pedal and pushing off. To him that proved only one thing – poor bikemanship – a pure sign of an eegit. I lost the rag – told him to show me. He said he wouldn't, but it was simple. Hold the bike on your right – place you're left foot on the inside pedal – push off and as the bike is moving – swing your right leg over the saddle. I said that was a stupid way – he said it was the only way. It developed into a shouting match – I was shouting – he was quiet and smirking. I hate that. Eventually, when I was tired shouting, he took the bike and with his left foot on the inside pedal, he pushed off and away – if it hadn't been for the row that preceded this event, I might have stood and admired his grace and poise. I might have been taken back to a time when he was young and in full flight – off to some dance in Corranary with my mother on the cross-bar – but I wasn't. All I could see was my fifty-three-year-old father on a black shiny bike with a big blow-horn on the handle-bars. I started to laugh and told him he looked ridiculous – my mother laughed a different laugh.

On a Monday in April, I set off for the Rough Hill – it took twenty minutes on the bike. I was early. Tommy Reilly was a young man in his early thirties. He had a fine farm – a so called 'Master-Farmer' – but he also had a recently set up furniture business. It was mostly dedicated to the new-fangled idea of a fitted kitchen. Up until recently, most houses had a dresser or the kitchen cabinet – but since the seventies and the arrival of a book called 'Bungalow Bliss' – the face of rural Ireland had changed. New houses were springing up everywhere. The day of one and a half and two-story farmhouses was gone. Bungalows were the thing – bungalows with big windows, hallways and huge kitchens were fashionable and cheap to build and they needed fitted kitchens. Tommy was ahead of his time, but his workshop wasn't.

He lived beside his farm with his young wife, Carmel and their two young boys. It was a modest country house. On the opposite side of the house from the farmyard, was a tiny building – once a pig house. This was our workshop for now. I had only met Tommy the once, when I asked about the job – I had been told all sorts of stories and warned by the messengers of doom, that he was tough – gruff and he mightn't pay. Well, I liked him – from the word go. He had a business to run and I had a wage to earn and we both pulled our weight. He didn't know it, but he was a natural teacher. I worked hard; I learned; I rode my bike and ate more sandwiches than was natural. My time in that place stood to me great, but there were other things afoot: girls, football, farming, dreaming, daring, dating, dancing, chancing and not enough sleeping. I was always twenty minutes early for work and I worked an extra ten minutes till it was ten-past-six. The weekends were bliss.

I went home one evening and there was a book on the table. This was one of the most unlikely sights you could expect to find in our house. We didn't have books – we didn't read books and we were never encouraged to give them any credence. My mother did succumb to the charms of a lad selling encyclopedias one time and that was used against her on many occasions. They were kept in the parlour with everything else we didn't need. On inspection, this book on the table was not for any pleasure purposes – not so bad. It was a 'Bungalow Bliss' book – a book of plans and drawings - some of the most up-to-date buildings on the planet – of course they were. The Auld Lad had finally given in to the notion of building a house.

My sister Margaret had deserted us by this time – like me, she had spent enough days at school – a lot more than me, in fairness. She had got a job in the Civil

Service – one of the best things that could happen to a rural family at the time – out from getting a calf to suck. She was happy out. She worked in the department of posts and telegraphs – that was our only claim to fame – for now. Because of her lofty position in Dublin we applied for the phone. That time there was a waiting list and a waiting time of up to two and a half years for a phone. We got ours almost right away and we didn't go for your normal run-of-the-mill black phone – we went for a beige one – or ivory to give it it's official description. We were on a runaway train to Poshville – except that we were still using the pots under the bed. I had at last gained control of my bladder, but phone or no phone – I still had to use the pot or the outside toilet. Bath time had changed too – the little iron tub had long since become a flowerpot and we now washed ourselves as best we could with a basin of water from the tank and a sponge.

In the middle of all this, my mother decided to make me and Kevin go to a dance. She was afraid that we might get like some of the neighbours and settle for Wonder Woman of a Tuesday, rather than using our own super-powers of a Saturday night in Bawn or Drumshanbo. It was a cross-over time in the dancing scene. The '60's and '70's had been embodied by the showband era – live bands in country halls doing cover versions of Elvis and Chuck Berry. That was now coming to an end. The rural dance halls were not going to be able to compete with hotels and bigger venues with their bar licenses and disco music. We had no interest in pubs or licensing laws and less interest in music. I had eased off the heavy metal and disco scene, since I lost the run of myself at the school hop. Kevin was more worried about getting another few cows to milk, than any slinkering around after women. But Mammy was worried that we might get odd and so we were sent to the 'Wonderland' dance hall in Bawn one Sunday night. There were dances in the Wonderland on Saturday and Sunday nights. Saturday was a good night when everyone was out – Sunday was more of a 'country' night and there was usually a fight and very few girls.

We got down with the Lees. I never knew me and Kevin were such good friends – we didn't want to leave each other that night. We paid our money and nudged our way in. We stood at the back in our two Mass jumpers and fell deep into our own thoughts. I was fifteen – this was 1980 – I loved nice round figures, but where was I? This could easily be a retirement home – the only sexually transmitted disease in the Wonderland was woodworm. We went to the mineral bar. There was Orange, Cidona or Cavan Cola – there was wafer snack, biscuit snack or Tayto crisps. There was a hole in the roof and it was raining. The place was full of drips and only one hole. Then Kevin took off. He knew Mammy would be asking did he dance, so he was going to give her a positive answer. He headed for a fairly plain one – good move I thought – go on Kevin! He got her at the first attempt. She was desperate and Kevin was good-looking and kind.

I didn't try any women – they were all a bit old and parcelled up looking. Hair-do's and paint and tied in the middle with belts – rings of fat above and below their tightened waists. I decided that Kevin getting a woman would be enough good tidings to bring back to Mammy, I could now relax and think about where we might build the new house.

There was never any consideration given to the idea that we might get a proper builder to build the house. No – the Auld Lad had built the byre when we were small. Mammy handed him the blocks with one hand and knitted with the other. Now he had two big sons and one of them was a carpenter and the other one, dancing below in Bawn. What more could you want to build a house

CHAPTER 35

Bench Saw Dreams

I lay on the saw-bench. I just had to lie down for ten minutes and close my eyes. It was lunchtime and I had an hour to myself. The first thing was to turn on the radio – Larry Gogan would be playing the Top Twenty – then I could have another go of sandwiches – then I needed to rest. It was Monday. I'd a match the day before – with the Juniors. I had been marked by a hairy lad from Bornacoola – the first thing he did, was spat in my face. I knew right away, he mustn't have been up to much, otherwise he wouldn't resort to spitting. That was a tough match and then at bedtime – as my father said – we went off to a dance in Granard, nearly forty minutes away.

The Lees – Mícheál and James had the use of the father's car – a Fiat Mirafiori – lovely yoke! That was our mode of transport to the Granada Ballroom in Granard. We went more for the spin than anything else. It was a fierce spot in it's time, but time caught up with

280 | SEAMUS O'ROURKE

the Granada Ballroom. It had also caught up with some of the ones going to it. It was usually a country band of a Sunday night – a small crowd and little in the way of excitement. You weren't even guaranteed a row in the Granada of a Sunday night.

The jump-suit was big at the time – there was one in Granard had three of them. She used to wear them on alternate nights – pink, blue and grey – they were all the same make. She must have got a bargain somewhere in some boutique – they were getting popular too. This girl was very dependable – she was always there – she would always dance, if you asked her. She'd never stay on – because we never asked her to and wouldn't want her to. Micheál Lee – who was Micky Lee at the dances – he was all micky at the dances – he said she was a nice lassie – that she might have stayed on with him one night – if he had coaxed her. Thank God he didn't – then we'd have no one to dance with. The best thing about the Granada, apart from the spin up in the car, was that there was a chip-van outside and it was never busy. It did horrid bad chips and burgers, but it saved us going up the town. Often, you'd have a pain the next day from the burger and eating so quick. It'd be three in the morning when we'd get home – if no one got a woman. God knows what time it'd be, if we ever did.

I don't know why we went to Granard of a Sunday night – I always suffered the next day. I didn't drink till I was twenty, so there was no hangover – but there was nothing else either – I was looking for a girl of my own age – I was the only fifteen-year-old going to the

Granada or the Wonderland or the Mayflower. I was desperate for something that I wasn't getting – I wasn't sure of what that was, but it was more than a burger and a choice of jump-suits.

My only fellow-employee at Reilly's was George. George was one careful carpenter – he held his work hostage for days on end. He had spent some time in England and that's the way they did it there. I didn't have the same sort of patience – but he taught me lots and I ploughed on. We didn't have hi-tec machinery, but Tommy Reilly of the Rough Hill had great know-how and drive. He was meticulous in his standards and it was a perfect place to learn my trade. The only thing was – it was quiet and not just at lunchtime. Often, Tommy and George would head off fitting and I was left to paddle the canoe. I revelled in the work – making sure there was a mountain of it done before they got back – but it was quiet and it was just me and three-quarters of a loaf of sandwiches and a calendar full of naked girls.

There was this calendar sponsored by a tool company. Every month a different girl with a different tool. Tools and parts of women that I'd never seen before. My favourite month was June – she stood – bare chested – drill in hand – looking straight at me. A far cry from Saint Patrick and a crowd of clatty snakes at his feet. I knew who I'd buy a drill off.

"Did you get paid?" – that was the only thing my father asked me about work. He was happy enough, if I was happy enough and getting paid. It was a mad dash

home on the bike every evening after work. The dinner was sucked in and off I'd go to training or a match – there was always some team in action – under 16 – minor – under 21 – junior and what would happen if I got on the County panel?

Me and Kevin headed off to a County Minor Trial – he was the right age and I was the right size. This was an exciting day – we both loved football and we were well aware of the great honour it was to play for your county. We got on well. We had to wait till the Leitrim Observer came out on Wednesday to see if we had made the panel. The Auld Lad said I was too young – that they'd never put a fifteen-year-old on an under 18 team. He was wrong – there it was in the paper the next Wednesday. The two Rourkes on the County. It was a long time since we first went to the field in front of the house. Me and my brother and a disfigured leather ball – the basic skills we practiced then, were the same skills we needed now. For now, football was kind and generous and loyal and we were so proud. This was to be another evening taken up with football – less help to do the things and us thinking of building a house.

The Auld Lad bought a digger – he had it this while, he was starting to make a fist of it. He had part of the field over from the house destroyed with him practicing with this digger – rootin' – pucking sods about with a shoring bucket. It was hard to get time with the hay and turf, but now he was getting used to the levers. He was in his ally. One Saturday morning, I was still in bed – exhausted from the week at work and peddling me bike and going to matches and not getting much sleep. There was the sound of the digger going by the window. It was the Auld Lad – taking the machine out of the practice yard and into the real world, but what job has he lined up for it?

When I got up the digger was sitting in the field in front of the house. What was it doing in the calf field? Our football field – our lovely field with the big ash tree in it. This was the site for our new house. It took a minute to sink in. I suppose it made sense. Breakfast was quiet that morning – it was the start of something new and exciting and about time too. But, it was also the end of something and the moment didn't go unnoticed. When we finished our boiled eggs, we sat and looked out the window towards the road – soon that view would be no more. Then we went to line out the new house.

There had been much debate about the type of house we'd build. The Auld Lad wanted to build a nice straight house – by that he meant a house with a straight roof – no L – no bits going off skew ways and making it difficult for the builder. We should have listened to him, but we didn't. Everyone bar him, wanted an L shaped bungalow – just a jutty-out bit at the front – just for cosmetic reasons – which was a very poor reason in my father's book. We got our way and the Auld Lad never quit complaining about this Bloody L.

We got out the builder's line and a few stakes and the Auld Man got up on the digger. He bogged the bucket of the machine into the good field in front of the house and the new house was under way. Would this be a new beginning or like some past projects, would it be a false dawn? The answer is – it started slow and then went on and on and on. We put in the foundation and that had to settle – for a year and then the building finally began and then the roof and the Bloody L and then all the rest. Each stage staggered around farm work and play.

Daddy was part of the management team with the Juniors. Sean Heslin, a former Aughavas and Leitrim great was the manager. Kevin was seventeen and a corner-back. I was fifteen and playing as a half forward. We won the whole thing – the Championship and the League and something else – it all went over my head a bit – I just wanted to play ball. Men cried, that day, when we won the Championship – and drank and talked. I saw the Auld Lad hugging all round him, but he never came near me – I was glad. I wouldn't know what to do, if he came near me with a hug. The art of hugging was not practiced in our house.

In September, Margaret invited me and Kevin up to Dublin, to stay for the weekend and go to the All-Ireland football final. This was fierce exciting – going to Croke Park – the mecca of our game. The night before we went up, I got lucky with one from Aughavas – I met her at a dance in Ballinamore – she near sucked the face off me. I went off to Dublin in great order. Margaret's bed-sit was on the North-Circular road. On the Saturday, she brought us to this dance at the National Ballroom – I got another woman there – from

Tipperary. She was a nurse and a good bit older than me – I'd say I could have learned things that night, if I had opened her at the right page. I'd had my fill the night before and here was another menu sitting in front of me – I just had the soup.

We got wet at the match – Kerry bet Roscommon and that wasn't great – but it was great to be there and add fuel to our dreams. And then we had to head home.

I was fit for the saw-bench, the next day at work – between the shenanigans with the two women and the up and down to Dublin, I was dying for a half hour's lying on the saw-bench. September on the calendar wasn't a patch on what I'd been through over the weekend – no matter what way she held the pencil.

CHAPTER 36

High Seas

I stood frozen on the 9 x 3 timber – I was never so afraid – the blood had drained from my face and my brain. I wanted this to be over – I wanted to be on the ground. Tommy Reilly was building a factory in Carrigallen – he had it up to the wall plates – all he had to do now, was put in a few purlins and she was ready for the roof. He brought me in to help. I was a great worker – there was nothing I wouldn't do – like go up 30ft off the ground without rope, rail nor harness. The highest I had ever been off the ground was when I was jumping for a ball at football. Tommy told me to grab the end of a plank and he took the other end and then away with him up a ladder and me up another and then he starts walking up a truss and what could I do, only go up after him. We never said no to anyone – especially when it involved work. The next thing, I'm above on the roof of Tommy Reilly's new factory and I was never so afraid in all my life and this roof didn't even have a Bloody L.

I saw Tommy's wife, Carmel drive in on the site with tea. Thank God for Carmel and the tea. I crawled down like a frightened snail. It was only a short respite, but a welcome one. That's when I should have announced my reluctance at falling to my death – but when you're sixteen and on sixty quid a week and it's March 1981 – you should be willing to float on air.

The house at home was three blocks high... this good while. We didn't know what height to put in the windows – it was a slow, stop, slow operation. The Auld Lad was fierce afraid of getting it wrong – and he was right to be. He called into every site around the country – looking to see the way they were doing it – then he'd decide against that way and pause for a week while he consulted Nostradamus. Meanwhile I was getting used to heights in Carrigallen.

The Football Club decided to go to London on a trip to celebrate the Junior final victory the year before. This would incorporate a game and a social and seeing the sights. That was the official line. The truth was it was going to be a mighty session of drink and sex – not a place you'd send a sixteen-year-old, but I had my own money now and no one was going to stop me. Kevin would go too. I had got on great with Tommy Reilly – at least up until now and working so high above sea-level. The £25 a week to start with wasn't great money, but in fairness to him – he shot it up well, when he saw that I was committed and useful. Now £60 a week for a sixteen-year-old was great money and me living at home. I started paying a few quid for my keep and putting the rest by – saving for a car. *"Do you need a car?"*, the Auld Lad would say. Of course I needed a car.

There were young lads flying up and down our road in lovely cars – Packie Smith; Hugh Joseph Maguire – all young men – all working – all with their own cars. There was no one pounding away on a 'Rudge' bike! Cycling to and from work sounds idyllic and it was some days, but very often it was raining and cold and a pure pain in the backside. I could out sprint tractors of the time, but locals in their cars asked for no better craic, than to come up behind me and toot their horn and beckon me to go faster and fool that I was – I would. I was fed up of rain and puddles and pity from hoors in cars. Kevin was driving the Escort. Sometimes, when it was our turn, we'd collect the Lees and go to Bawn or Drumshanbo or Granard – it didn't seem right going off to a dance in the same car that brought us to Mass. It was always the same result. We'd get there late and come out empty handed – Jesus wasn't one for staying on with lads from Drumeela and the women we chanced must have been closely related.

There was a lot of talk at football practice about London and what we'd do to London, when we went over on this trip. The Auld Lad said we'd want to be careful – a bunch of mad Irish lads might not be overly welcome in London in1981. He was right of course, but me and Kevin passed no remarks. We had a boat journey to contend with first.

As far as I was concerned, my brother was invincible – strong as an ox – brave, bold, determined, conscientious and honest. Half way across the Irish sea, he was a sort of a dull greenish colour. I was feeling how he looked. We couldn't eat – that's how sea-sick we were. We could never not eat. The boat trip across the Irish sea reminded us that God was in charge and to behave ourselves.

The 1980 Junior team and our entourage were easily spotted around London. There were fifty of us – players, young and not so young; officials, but not my dad and then a few people from around the parish, who took advantage of the cheap excursion to the English capital. We walked around together – all fifty of us. It was baking hot – but everyone had their coat on their arm in case it rained – and then everyone gawking into every shop - you'd think it was Mullan Market we were in. We were staying in Guest Houses, but we thought they were hotels. The first morning, one of our pranksters, Sambo Reilly, lined us up and like the pied piper – led us off to a very special place he'd found. No one asked any questions and we all ended up in a picture house, showing porn. There was a few rosary's said, but no one left, as we had already paid at the door. It was an education for most, especially for a sixteen-year-old, recovering from sea-sickness. I was just a whippersnapper with only two pairs of underpants.

That night, the older lads went on the beer. Me and Kevin were two of the few not drinking. We were focusing on the game the next day – we shouldn't have bothered. It was a sham. Some of our team were still drunk – all of the other team were definitely drunk or just the worst sober team ever to play the game. The non-drinkers won, but no one cared and suddenly, this trip that we had saved for – our first trip overseas – made little sense. The post-match lunch turned into another drinking session and then it was time to go out.

Going out in London is not like going out in Carrigallen – everything starts early and finishes early. We got the tail end of a dance in the Galtymore Ballroom and the tail end of the talent too. A well-endowed Duchess of Drunkenness, dragged me on to the floor for the National Anthem – it wasn't even the right National Anthem – she wanted to jive. I wouldn't be a jiver at the best of times. I stood to attention – she danced around me like I was a pole. I knew she'd be hard to shake off. It turns out her friends had befriended my friends – three members of our junior team – plans were afoot to go back to our Guest House. This was thin ice.

Opportunities were about to come tumbling into my lap and I wasn't ready. The lads had bought carry-outs and we were in a big sitting room – couples had formed and lights were dimmed – I wish I had paid more attention at the porn movie. Majella was from Tyrone and very drunk and I was very hungry. I knew I had half a sandwich in my room, but I was afraid to bring her there, in case she'd eat it. I decided to leave the sitting room to the more established players on our team and me and Majella went into the hall. She said we could do it on the stairs. I said, I'd rather not, that I wasn't good on heights. She seemed puzzled – she suggested she take off her top and then she did. She said I was a funny colour – I said I was very prone to sea-sickness – she asked what age I was – I lied – I said fourteen. She said, *"You're a bit young for sailing in this vessel"*, and she gathered up her plumage and went back into the sitting-room. I slunk off to bed.

As the summer progressed the new house was taking shape – any spare time was put into building blocks. These months were full; work and sometimes overtime; football; the house; the usual farm work; football and football again. I was now playing with the County Minors and under 16's. I was playing well and making a name for myself. The Auld Fella hadn't seen me play county. I don't know why and I never asked. Then one Wednesday evening, we were playing Cavan in an under 16 county game. It was just in the road – in Ballinamore – and the Auld Fella said he'd go. I was nervous. He brought me to the venue. I could feel his eyes on me the whole game – I was suffocated by his presence. I could hear his sighs and his tut's – not literally, but I knew he'd be unimpressed by my efforts – the harder I tried – the further away I was from what I wanted to achieve. I was pathetic that day and he had to be there to see me flounder. The great county man was a sham.

He tried to offer some constructive advice on the way home, but I just heard criticism and disappointment. How dare he, who never kicked a ball – tell me how to play the game. I hoped he would never come to another and he didn't, until I played bad again.

It probably didn't help that my father was a 'Glass is half empty', sort or that he had this fierce sense of realism or that he didn't want to patronize – but I couldn't go him watching me play football. What I did never satisfied him. He'd talk about this one and that – how well they played, but he never told me that. Not once did he say I played well. He told me one day, *"You weren't as bad today as I often saw you"*, and that was as good as it got. I was quickly becoming obsessed with what my father thought and I don't know why.

And if he wasn't going to like my playing – I didn't think much of his building. This house was taking forever and he was supposed to be an expert – he had built the byre – or did he? Maybe it was Mammy built the byre!

CHAPTER 37

Rock Bottom

The factory that me and Tommy Reilly had roofed in Carrigallen, wasn't really a factory, it was a shed. A fine big shed, yes, but the Carrigallen's called it a factory and it wasn't – that's townies for you. This fine shed on the outskirts of the town was finished and we were in. The 'Rough Hill' and working in the low pig house was no more. I was now cycling the four miles to Kivvy and it was exciting. We had a couple of new machines, loads of headroom and the future looked bright.

The house at home had got to the roof stage and this Bloody L. It was coming into winter, a perfect time to start roofing. The Auld Fella had bad circulation and his hands would go blue in cold weather – a day on a roof in November with a claw-hammer and a bag of nails was just the place for him and his bad humour. My carpentry skills did not include roofing or climbing or listening to a man complaining about *"This Bloody L"*.

When I was a few months into my job at Tommy Reilly's – I realised I wasn't signed up to an apprenticeship – it was just a job. We had a chat and he said he couldn't sponsor me, but if I wanted to do an apprenticeship, he wouldn't stop me. So, I decided to do my apprenticeship outside of work. My old school principle, Mick Duignan, was very helpful and I did my exams through the school. Therefore, I had to do all my theory and practical study in my own time. Strangely, I had never really studied before, and now here I was getting up at 6am to do just that. An AnCO certificate and a City & Guild qualification would be my reward. This, along with normal work and the new house and the football, helped fill out my day.

My social activities had taken a back seat, since the London trip. I wasn't exactly sure what had gone on there, but my confidence had taken a battering. I had been presented with an opportunity and I didn't take it. I couldn't blame the Auld Fella either. He wasn't on the stairs in London with me and Majella from Tyrone – shouting, *"Go on – ya boy ya"*. I had no one to blame, but me – and maybe I hadn't done the wrong thing – maybe I was right to not go sliding down the slippery slope of seduction. The only thing was, I might never get the chance again. Sixteen is not a great age for meeting a girl, if you're in South Leitrim in 1981.

Here I was – a County Man... Leitrim Young footballer of the year 1980... a working man with his own money... dressed to kill in Mullan Market fashion – and there was as much chance of meeting a girl as there was of meeting a Protestant at Mass. And then it happened and it was at Mass. Mass of all places – I saw this girl – a stranger – God must have sent her – she was tall and beautiful and enough to give a lad a bit of hope. I saw Michéal Lee going from Michéal to Micky in an instant – he was gawking over at her too, but what was he going to do in the chapel? There was no slow set at Drumeela ten o'clock Mass. I wasn't going to do anything either... for the time being – but at least, now I had hope. The Auld Fella said, *"That was a fine tall lassie at Mass today"* – good man Daddy – he had a good eye! He knew the mother – moved to Dublin years ago. Mammy said she was tall too – there was a fierce discussion about this one from Dublin and how tall she was.

We were having the tea and the bit to eat after we came home from Drumeela. It was a bitterly cold and wet November day. There was a time when we wouldn't work of a Sunday – unless we had hay down and it was going to rain – or if we had a cow calving or if the cows had got out, but normally if we had no hay down and it wasn't going to rain and there were no cows out or calving and apart from the usual doing the things – we wouldn't work of a Sunday – not till this new house started. There was a chance today, with the cold and the rain and the fact that me and the Auld Fella had fallen out over the angle of a cut on this Bloody L, that we might leave the work to one side for once – and watch 'The Little House on the Parie' and fall asleep like normal people of a Sunday. But no – as soon as we discussed the tall girl from Dublin, the Auld Lad went over to the range to warm his hands and I knew that could mean only one thing – up on the roof again – my heart sank.

What do you say to a tall girl from Dublin that you haven't met? You talk to her in your head – like you're in a film – the words all come out poetically and you say the right thing and she says the right thing and before you know it, you're in an embrace.

Or you're up a ladder with your Auld Fella. Up on a bloody roof of a Sunday with the hands falling off you, because you have the same bad circulation as him. Not good for the day-dreaming. Still, it's nice to have a warm thought in your head and a little dream to slide in alongside it. Romantic notions never knocked anyone off a ladder in November.

The valley, where one roof joins another at right angle, is a devil to get right. The amount of work entailed would build another house – or so my Father thought. He wasn't wrong – we spent weeks footherin' around at this damn thing. It didn't mean we had a bigger house – just a slightly different house – until some of our neighbours built the same house and so all we really got was frustration and moaning and very cold and blue hands. By the second day of Christmas, it was ready for slates. Christmas wasn't the same without Santy or childishness – so, on St. Stephens Day 1981, I sat on the felt and nailed on slates. It was cold and frosty, but it was dry and calm – by the time the New Year came, we were almost there – with the roof. How much longer would this take. I was near ready for my bath.

At least with County football, we got to play in places where we could shower after games – there weren't many football grounds in Leitrim with this facility, but the centenary of the Gaelic Athletic Association was coming up in two years' time and lots of clubs, including Carrigallen were striving for new pitches and dressing rooms.

In March '82, I turned seventeen. In April, I passed my driving test. Everyone knew what was coming next – I announced I was buying a car. Imagine a second car on the street – an ivory telephone and still nowhere to poo. I could tell Daddy was as excited as I was – he loved cars and garages and kicking tyres. We scanned the Leitrim Observer and the Anglo Celt for yokes and drew circles around certain ones. And then one Saturday – all work ceased on the bungalow and we blissfully headed car hunting. He took on the role of sensible, realistic parent, but secretly he was just as keen as me to go sporty and get a car that I could enjoy. I bought a three-year-old Opel Kadett Coupe – it was red with lots of chrome and me and the Auld Lad looked like the Beverley hillbillies driving home.

There was other excitement that spring – our County Minor team were showing real promise! A false dawn according to my father. He wasn't begrudging success – he was being realistic. Realism in Leitrim at the time, was to assume the worst – multiply that by two – subtract all good fortune and chance and then add extreme caution. Some of us still had hope however and dedication. By the summer, we had beaten Mayo and were in a Connacht Final – the biggest game in Leitrim for years. Of course, this had always been part of my plan. To win Connacht and then play in Croke Park. It was the best thing that had happened in my life to this point. Now for the worst.

The day before this most important of matches – I drove to Cavan town and bought a double cassette tape called, 'Hits of the Sixties'. It was a horrid price compared to Mullan Market, but I wanted something to take my mind off the game. It didn't. I drove around all that day listening to music and thinking about nothing only the game. This is my chance – this is my time. Don't let it slip – I'm on the cusp of success. History is about to be made – I was exhausted from thinking about it. I was far better had I spent the day on the roof fighting with the Auld Lad.

That Connacht Minor Final appearance of 1982 was a disaster. I, and a few others, conspired to over think the occasion – to arrive at the most definitive hour in our young lives, only to – as my mother would say – *"Shit on the eggs"*. I was completely drained – emotionally and physically and that was before I even took to the field. We lost by a point. My father summed it up best, when he said... nothing. – He completely ignored the fact that the match took place at all. Of course, anything he might have said would have been taken up wrong, but... still. I was inconsolable and I didn't deal with it very well. I fell into a state of numbness and St Patrick and all the saints and snakes in heaven couldn't help. I needed time and I didn't get time, but I got the next best thing – a real dirty derby match with Drumreilly – it came the following week. Sport is like that... it's like an alcoholic partner who pushes you to the brink – abuses you – and then brings you flowers. We loved playing Drumreilly – they were just up the road from our house – this was the team I had followed when there was no team in Carrigallen – some of my heroes played for Drumreilly, but when it came to the local derby, me and my brother put on our 'Hats of Hatred' and went to war. Of course they shouted – *"You didn't do it for Leitrim last Sunday"*, or even less subtle, *"Go on Rourke, ya Bollix ya - you're no good, you were never any good and you never will be"*. We won the match and the Auld Fella was happy, but not with me – how could he be happy with me? I had let everyone down the Sunday before. I threw myself into work and football and driving with my elbow out the window.

CHAPTER 38

Packie

I was proud of the round-about way I was doing my apprenticeship. Most businesses would send you off to college for blocks of three months at a time to learn your trade. Those who did it that way, mostly learned how to dodge work rather than do it more efficiently. I was learning by doing and doing what I could to help with this new house – I was getting fed up being a good boy for staying at home and helping with the now – not-so-new bungalow that might not be finished by the time we were all grown up and gone.

Rural Ireland in the early '80's for a seventeen-year-old was like being covered in glue – everywhere you went, some part of your home life or your community life was stuck to your shoe or in my case... my forehead. Sometimes, I wished I could clear it all away and be cool for a day, but that was never going to happen – the glue was everywhere.

It was at Mass – we congregated at the chapel gate and someone said, *"How is all your crew?"*. In the shop

303

they said *"That's the way Seamus, you never thought of going away, aren't you great – you must be a fierce help at home – how is the lovely new house coming on?"* We went to social dances in the hall – benefit dances – dinner dances – dances with a buffet supper – *"Anyone for the last dance"*. What do you say to people at these things? *"Big Crowd..."* *"Great turnout..."* *"How's your mother?"* *"That was an awful shower of hailstones – did you'se get that? We were just sitting down to the tea and the heavens opened..."*

All I can remember is being very polite for about three years – like I was in a glass cabinet full of very fragile glass people – glass figurines everywhere and glass goblets and sherry glasses held by little old glass women that never farted or frowned – just smiled politely and wished God's Blessings on you and all at home. Wouldn't you just love to take a big side of beef and wallop the whole lot into smithereens. Explode before you implode, even if it meant spending the rest of your life going about with a dust pan and brush.

My mother was a great cook – and the less ingredients the better – she had taken a job waitressing in the Hotel in Carrigallen – the Killbracken Arms. It was run by Maura and Alfie Harte. Maura was the chef and my mother liked her style – Mrs. Harte would do as much as three in the kitchen. My mother didn't cook in there, but she lifted and carried and waited tables like no other. She did, however, broaden her culinary skills and now that Kevin was a fulltime farmer – she had a chance to experiment and recreate some of the hotel's cuisine. We sat in and ate whatever was laid before us.

Then she took a job in the clothing factory in Ballinamore. She was almost forty and had never worked in a nine-to-five job before. McCartin's Clothing factory in Newtown was closed at the time and so Ballinamore was the next best thing. All of this was her way of contributing towards the new house, as if she hadn't contributed enough already. Now she hadn't time to peel a spud.

On the first day, she waited at the foot of the road for Doherty's mini-bus. Like a frightened schoolgirl she climbed on with her lunch and twenty-two years of farming experience – twenty-two years of hardship and frustrations – twenty-two years of working against the grain, where no man, child or beast could faze her and now for eight weeks of her life she would suffer an emotional torture and embarrassment – which, ultimately, sucked the life and confidence from within her.

We were poor support – we were her family – we should have gone in and called out whatever hoor was causing this – or was this caused by anything other than a life hidden away in the bushes? Maybe she wasn't ready for the big bad world! She was forty – I was seventeen – maybe, I wasn't ready either.

After eight weeks – Newtown clothing had reopened and my mother transferred as a fully trained seamstress and she never looked back. Her new environment was a haven in comparison to the previous eight weeks and she thrived – it's never too late. She was a working woman, but still feed calves and waitressed in the Killbracken Arms.

The hotel had a couple of weddings a week and every aforementioned dance was held in their function room. Rural Ireland was staying afloat by drowning its sorrows. There were seven pubs in Carrigallen at the time – all in full swing – all full of auld lads who were better footballers than those of us trying to play... or so it went.

I took on to do the carpentry in the house – the only things we didn't do ourselves were the plastering, the plumbing and the electrics. I hung the doors and the second fixings – made wardrobes for the bedrooms and then the centre piece – a solid-wood kitchen. During all this, my father stood back and played second fiddle – just like I had done, not many years before when we made the press in Druminchin. He would soon be fifty-five – the age I am now as I write these words. Like me, he had his failings and his failures and now he had come to a point in his life where he felt he should stand back and let others have a go. He was disappointed for me and my football limitations and would have loved if I had succeeded – he might have even stolen a little of that success for himself – but he was a generous man with human qualities way beyond those of mine – it's just we never learned to communicate – with each other or even with ourselves – neither of us exactly sure of what we wanted or where we were headed.

One weekend, my mother took into a flitter and cleaned out the new house – it had been going on for about two and a half years and still wasn't near completion – but it could still do with a good tidy. She and Geraldine, who was now fourteen and with the same zest for work – swept and carted to the tip – for the first time the house was taking shape and gave us renewed energy. That Sunday morning, after Mass – Packie McKeever came calling.

Packie was a unique and wonderful individual who lived just down the road in Druminchin, a next-door neighbour of my mother when she lived there. There were nine in his family, six boys and three girls. He and his twin brother, Dan were the youngest. The McKeevers were all highly intelligent, including Packie, only Packie was missing a few strands in the thought process. This meant he could be very astute at times and at times, very off the mark. His underlying quality was one of generosity and kindness and he possessed a childlike quality in his comprehension. He didn't call often, but when he did, he usually caused a stir.

"Well Packie!"

"Aye, I just called up to see the house"

"Come in..."

"Youse are getting on well – I'd say it's dry, is it?"

"It is..."

"What was wrong with the other one?"

"The other house?"

"Aye, it was always a nice warm house"

"Still is..."

"But sure, I suppose, if yez weren't happy in it..."
"No, it's just there was no bathroom..."
"But Jim, your mother had no bathroom or your father"
"That's true I suppose..."
"You'll miss the tank at the side of the range..."
"We will...
"And the soft water..."
"Aye..."
"At least you'll be closer to the road!"

Packie looked about for a while and then walked off without word nor blessing and we were left to sift through his observations. The old house was a good house – just not good enough for us anymore – we needed a bathroom... and what else? Could we not have built our bathroom ten years ago and be free from debt and desperation. Not have my mother heading off at the age of forty – trying to fit in with young ones my age. Complicating an uncomplicated life and for what? Bungalow Bliss my Granny!

And right on cue – Granny arrived with her entourage – Aunt Peggy and Uncle Bernie. Granny didn't often come visiting – she was eighty-six now and using up most of her energy on Bingo and prayer. She had appeared a few times when we were in the early stages of the house – the early stages had gone on for a while. She remarked, *"At least it's gone beyond the string stage?"* – the string stage she was referring to was when the outline of the house remained pegged out for those couple of years. Granny might have been getting old, but she still liked to get her cut in. Peggy and Bernie were more interested in the nuts and bolts of the build. We were just fed up talking about it.

We all sat in at the table then and Mammy and Geraldine presented hotel standard food in O'Rourke standard portions. Geraldine was now working in the Killbracken Arms with Mammy – one as big a glutton for work as the other. After we had talked about the lovely ham and the beetroot from the garden and the lettuce, which were good that year – we paused; took a breath and tore into the grub. Don't talk with your mouth full – don't talk at all – you can talk when you're done eating... and then we were – done eating – it never took too long. Granny looked out the front window. Instead of the view that once was – the white picket fence – the big old ash tree and the two piers at the road, she saw the fifty-foot backwall of a monstrosity and sadness filled her eyes. What had we done?

CHAPTER 39

Driving Off

When the occasion arises, that you must look at what you have through someone else's eyes, you can be shocked at what you see. All throughout our young lives, we grumbled and groaned about our lot – the hardship and the consistency of it – never once did we get a break – never once were we lucky and win a holiday or a car or a house. The two white piers at the road was where our world began or ended – depending on which way we were going and the mood we were in. The bus to the outside world would stop and pick us up or drop us off – but the bus never took us away completely. We went to school or the clothing factory in Ballinamore or we waited for Patsy Wrynn's tooting horn as he came around McCaffery's turn – he brought us on our greatest folly – football. We went to Tuam and Carrick and Castlebar, but never far enough to detach ourselves from home. At home we snuggled into reality and found comfort in what others thought unjust.

I drove off down the lane in my shiny bright, chrome speckled, red sports machine. I was seventeen – my body, tall and lean and tight – my shirt white and my Levi's might have been 501's. It could have been the end of a movie – I drive out those gates one last time – leave the drudgery and bureaucracy behind and become great. But instead I was only going to Mullan Market to buy tapes.

I had put a stereo into the car – well I had put in two – the first one only played one song. These stereos were got cheap in the market. – We'd spend days wrestling with the dash – trying to put a stereo where there was no place for a stereo – but that's what lads of my vintage did. These cars had no slots for music machines or speakers – and although there was no car-crime in Leitrim – no stealing cars or joy-riding; no car vandals roaming the valleys looking for cars – we conspired to ransack our own cars at the weekends with hacksaw blades and cable wire and insulation-tape or just sellotape. Beatin' stereos into cars that would rather not have Dire Straits Greatest Hits booming out the side doors and shaking the dash to shreds.

None of this was fun – we had an image in our head – you're driving with your baby(girlfriend)... (your really lovely girlfriend) – it's eight o'clock on a summer's evening – that was the usual pick-up time, if you had a steady girlfriend – you'd pick her up and leave rubber on her street – take off like you were driving a Ferrari – give her brothers and sisters a wee toot of your musical horn and then off down the lane like a rocket. Most of the good-looking women lived along the road, but the ones I was courting would live in a fairly long lane. Then, when you'd get to the open road and after you told her that her father's meadows were looking good this year – you'd nonchalantly reach over and turn on the Dolby Audio, rich, clear stereo sound of The Eagles or Eric Clapton... she'd sink back into the passenger seat and you wouldn't have to say a word till the tape needed turning or it got tangled and you'd have to pull over and take out the pencil.

That was the idea – but even getting a tiny red light inside in the contraption was a major achievement when you're an apprentice cabinet maker... not working in your own field. *"Hook it directly to the battery"* – that was my father's only advice– this led to more flat batteries and pushing matches! You spend an hour pulled in by the old quarry with your baby (the girlfriend) – kissing and cuddling and licking her ear and then when it's time to bring her back up the lane – the car won't start. It's not every woman wants to push that early in the relationship – but it's not a bad way of finding out if she'd be any good around the farm. Sometimes – if the mood was right – you mightn't bother pushing or jump-starting – you might just continue the fondling and the footherin' and the ear-licking. Twisting the knob on the side of the seat – gently lowering yourself and herself into position. It was a bit like the putting in of the stereo in the first place.

We never managed surround sound. We had four speakers alright – two up front or in the door and two in the back window – all with the same mono sound, because we didn't know our left rear from our front right – which wire was which? Red or blue or white or brown – and every Sunday spent in Mullan Market, trying to find new music.

This Sunday in August, I was feeling grown up – I had my cool-ish image packed into the rear-view mirror – my Connacht Final nightmare put out of my head and I was cruising – whatever nonsense was going on at home with the new house – it was not my problem – not today. Today it was just me and my car that I had worked so hard to get – my hit and miss stereo that wanted so badly to hop out of the dash – the sun was shining and the window was down, but this facade didn't last for long.

At the bottom of Druminchin lane – Packie McKeever was looking for a lift – thumbing as he did – he wouldn't know one car from the other – so driving by was no big crime. I drove by, left him standing along the road – someone else would come along – this was my time. As I came down by Frank the Tailor's – I thought of Packie again – I liked him and enjoyed his simple turn on life. I thought of going back, but I kept going – Jackson Brown was in the middle of a seven-minute song – was there really need for it being so long? What if no one picked up Packie? At the corner in Newtown, I should have swung around, but I turned for Ballinamore – who did I think I was? At Derryniggan –

the 'Sharp' Stereo spat out Jackson Brown. Today the song would not be seven-minutes long. I spun around at Benny Rourke's and went back to pick up my neighbour. What was I trying to become? In spite of all the grooming – my hair, not much beyond the pudding-bowl – my after-shave searching for anything that was after being shaved – I was still covered in that glue – I was still from here – time I embraced it.

Packie had sat on the ditch along the road– a low ditch, grass growing up around him – looked like he was planted there. A circle of smoke from a Hamlet Cigar – a perfect image for a TV commercial! Here was a man in his own thoughts and surroundings – who was going whatever way his lift was going – it might be soon or not for a while, but he didn't care. He had his Hamlet Cigar. I pulled up and he smiled –

"Ah Seamus – I never know your car – it's very like young Smith's – which way are you going? I'll be with you some of the way... If you're not in a hurry, I'll smoke this before I get in – Aye... thanks very much for stoppin".

I told him there was no hurry – what rush was I in? I had a tendency at the time – when I was in the car – to let it be known that I was in a hurry – always impatiently revving. I had drove past Drumlea Chapel a few months before, when the Drumreillys were coming out from Mass – I was on my way to Ballinamore, to catch a bus to a county game. Suddenly surrounded by worshipers – I flew into a tizzy – elbow out and revving – I darted from side to side, trying to avoid the throng.

316 | SEAMUS O'ROURKE

It wasn't so much the ones with the prayer books and rosary beads, it was the others. There's nothing so heedless as a heathen after a long Mass. They were everywhere and I should have surrendered, but I didn't, I kept going – I left tyre-marks on the road and a cloud of dust in my wake. The next day, Tom Mimna informed me that I had ran over the Master's toe. The Master was Pat Conefrey – local National School teacher and former Leitrim Footballer – a better man than I would ever be – a man whose big left toe had more craft and character than my whole ancestry put together – but it just happened to be in the wrong place.

Packie finished his cigar and sat in – I turned at Druminchin Lane – we headed for Newtown again – I was happier now – all the better for my change of heart. Packie would have been none the worse for my drive-by, but I would.

At Christmas that year – we spent our last year in the old house – My father was fifty-five – my mother, forty – Margaret was twenty-one – Kevin, twenty – Geraldine was fourteen and I was seventeen – we were all grown up now or at least it looked that way – we bought each other grown-up presents and we had grown-up things to eat. The farm still overshadowed our daily lives, including Christmas Day. The new house was tired of being new and unlived in – it would be almost a year before we'd move in. Those who saw it in its shiny newness said it was like 'Fuckin Dallas' – the highest compliment that could be paid at the time.

It was strange and great to be able to have a shower or bath or go to the toilet indoors. We always had an out-door loo – it's still there. The wind would cut you from under the door – we went there for the obvious, but also – to sulk – to hide – to calm down and to cry.

We had a Mass in the house when we finally moved in. My Uncle Father Kevin loved saying Mass in houses – still does – you get a different angle when you bring God a céilí. We all had to come up with a prayer during 'prayers for the faithful'. I'll always remember my brother's offering – he never failed to articulate what was right. He said – *"I hope we're as happy here as we were in the old house"*. We all hoped that.

Acknowledgments

To *Julie Smith* for supporting, copy editing and proofing. My three children, *Jessica*, *Thiernan* and *Séalin* – for their love and support, and for making all things worthwhile. To my Grandson, *Fionn*, who won't remember his interruptions, but I will... and they were mostly welcome. To *Patricia Ledwith*, who always said I should write a book... and now I have. *Con Collins* (Once of Collins Press) for suggesting I write a memoir – that was eight years ago. To *Seanán Brennan* for his beady eye. To my teachers along the way – they had their work cut out, but they left their mark. To my family who star in this book... my father – *Jim*; my mother – *Pauline*; my brother – *Kevin;* my two sisters – *Margaret* and *Geraldine*... Thank you! Growing up with you, in the place we called home, didn't scar me, it just etched my name and address firmly on the band of my underpants. To all the people mentioned in this book who are gone to their eternal reward – you brought such fun and laughter into our lives. May you rest in peace.

Everything for this book was sourced locally – the author and the story. *Ronan Ward* at www.homebird.ie designed the cover – *Turloch Dolan* and his staff at www.harvestmoonprinting.com looked after printing and loads of people said *"Well, fair play to ya!"*. I'm a very lucky boy and this was my early life of *Standing in Gaps*.

About the Author

Seamus O'Rourke is an actor, poet and playwright. He has written fifteen stage plays including four one-man-shows. He has 'A Book of Poems, Recitations and Good Ones'. He's widely known for his simple storytelling – capturing rural Irish life in a way that both amuses and affects. All books, plays, CD's and an audio download of this memoir can be found on his website:

Website: www.seamusorourke.com

Twitter: @seamus_orourke

Facebook.com/seamusorourkeactor

318